GOLF FOR A LIFETIME!

GOLF FOR A LIFETIME!

BY BOB TOSKI WITH JERRY TARDE

PHOTOGRAPHY BY STEVE SZURLEJ

A GOLF DIGEST BOOK

Published by Golf Digest/Tennis Inc.
A New York Times Company
495 Westport Avenue
Norwalk, Connecticut 06856

Trade book distribution by
Simon and Schuster
A Division of Gulf + Western Industries, Inc.
New York, New York 10020

First Printing
ISBN: 0-914178-49-0
Library of Congress: 81-83914
Manufactured in the
United States of America

Cover and book design by Dorothy Geiser.
Printing and binding by
Kingsport Press, An Arcata Company.

PHOTO CREDITS
All photographs by Steve Szurlej except:
p. 9, Sarazen, top, Wide World; bottom,
UPI; p. 40, Mike O'Brien; p. 42 and pp.
112-3, Larry Petrillo.

TABLE OF CONTENTS

1 GOLF FOR A LIFETIME!

I was 10 years old when Gene Sarazen came to town one summer day to play an exhibition with Babe Didrikson at the Northampton Country Club in Massachusetts, where my brother Ben was the assistant pro.

I'll never forget that day. Gene had on knickers and a long-sleeved shirt and tie, and Babe was wearing a long skirt with an anchor embroidered on it. They were quite a pair, the lithe and masculine Babe towering over dark-eyed, sleek-haired Gene. I remember standing on the second-story porch looking down at the two celebrities in awe. It was the first time I had ever seen great golfers.

I would never have dreamed in a million years that some day I'd play golf with Gene Sarazen. Actually, it didn't take a million years—just a little more than 40. At the first big senior pro tournament, the inaugural Legends of Golf in 1978, I found myself paired with Gene the first day. He still had on knickers, which by now were his trademark. Since he was the senior senior in the tournament, Sarazen was playing in the first group and he had the honor of driving off the first ball.

As Gene teed up, the announcer introduced him by telling practically his whole life story. As I listened, I started thinking back to when I had seen Sarazen that first time so long ago. I am an emotional person to begin with, so it wasn't long before the drama of the moment got to me. Finally, the announcer finished and Gene hit. When it was my turn, I needed a towel to wipe the tears away. I couldn't even see the ball when I hit it.

I bring up this story now because it shows what a lasting effect people can have on the lives of others. From the time of that childhood encounter, Gene Sarazen has been an inspiration to me. Now he's about become the patron saint of senior golf. As he approaches his 80th birthday, shooting his age more times than not, Gene proves that golf truly is a game of a lifetime.

In these pages, I would like to share with you the pleasure golf has brought into my life. Just as Sarazen inspired me, I hope to inspire you to improve your game so that you can enjoy your golf and live the rest of your life a happier person.

Fortunately, I have plenty of help. I'll be citing the example of many of my fellow senior professionals. This is not a book that teaches the concept of one person, but of many. The senior pros whom I quote, comment on and show photographs of, are my

Bob Toski and the patron saint of senior golf, Gene Sarazen, shown competing in 1932...and four decades later.

friends, but they're also independent and insightful thinkers about the game. If you've never had the chance to talk to Julius Boros or Sam Snead or Byron Nelson, this book will give you a glimpse of what has made them successful players and how, to varying degrees, they have been able to maintain this success into their senior years.

We first need to clear the air about the word "senior." Some people think "senior" means old and senile. Old is a state of mind. To me, senior denotes command and respect. A person is proud to be a senior officer in the military or a senior partner in a law firm or the senior diplomat in a delegation. It means that person is at the height of his or her career. Likewise, senior citizens deserve respect. And so do senior golfers.

Certainly nobody wants to get old. The trick is to learn how to handle this "revoltin' development," as comedian Jimmy Durante used to say, with grace. You won't see me moaning about getting old. As a matter of fact what I do is brag about it. At this writing I am 54, fit as many a man half my age, I believe, and playing golf like hell. Is my attitude wrong? I don't think so. I'm proud that I've been able to keep my body in shape. I feel sorry for anyone who takes a negative attitude about growing older, because that only makes him (or her) grow older faster.

Gene Littler has the perfect outlook on life. He's gone through some rough times, including a battle with cancer. He's learned to cope with age by thinking positive.

"The trick is never to give up playing like a kid. When I first learned the game, I just stepped up and hit the ball. But the more you play, the more complicated you try to make it. The trouble starts when you try to figure out the reason for a bad shot instead of going ahead—like a kid—and playing the next shot. You've got to keep thinking young."—Gene Littler

Up until a couple of years ago, most of the present senior tour players were living comfortable lives as club professionals, playing golf only on the weekends if that much. Then suddenly all of these tournaments for 50-year-olds and up were organized. I'll never forget the excitement of being reborn to competitive play. But quickly most of the "new" tour pros found out we weren't as good as we thought we were, and we were forced back to the practice tee. We hit balls, worked on the short game and exercised. Eventually, a glimmer of our old golfing selves showed through. The 75s we shot became 70s, and we were no longer ashamed to put our games on display.

"It was like being given a second chance. It was also an opportunity to put a lot of knowledge I gained over the years back to use in playing competitive golf. Not that I think I was getting decrepit, but this has been a great way to stay young."—Doug Ford

That first senior tournament, in which I played with Sarazen, was won by the team of Sam Snead and Gardner Dickinson. When Sam holed long putts to birdie the last three holes, we all tried to remember when he had ever played better.

If the current senior movement was sparked by one event it was the next Legends of Golf held in 1979. Julius Boros and Roberto de Vicenzo tied Tommy Bolt and Art Wall after the regulation 54 holes. The six-hole sudden-death playoff that followed, indelibly recorded by television, featured nine birdies—nine birdies in six holes!— and was won by Boros and De Vicenzo. I think it can be said that this single telecast made senior golf. It was unexpectedly, unbelievably dramatic. The fans had figured the old guys would be blowing two-footers and stubbing chip shots. But here they were knocking the flag down and holing putts from all over. They were like youngsters out there, wagging their fingers at one another, as if to say, "Match that shot, kiddo!" Damn, these pros really were still young. And, "you can still be young, too!" is the message that went out over the tube to a couple of generations of older golfers.

Senior golf to me has meant returning to competition, meeting my old competitive rivals and friends, trying to recapture the old touch and the old concentrated effort, producing shots under pressure, studying up on the other players' swings and noticing if they've maintained their superiority or slipped downhill, seeing if they've got fat or stayed skinny. These experiences—probably as much as anything in my life—have made me a better teacher.

Pride is our strongest motivation for improvement. It is the quality that makes Sam Snead, with six full decades behind him, continue to compete just as vigorously for a $5 nassau as for the U.S. Open.

Pride is also the reason other professionals, such as Ben Hogan, refuse to compete. Ben wants the public to remember him in all his greatness; he doesn't want to tarnish that image. That's a shame only because in my opinion it has deprived a generation of new golfers of seeing the great man play. What I don't think Hogan realizes is that the public would not care about the scores he made. I know from the many exhibitions I've given over the years that, if you hit one fantastic shot, that shot will be remembered long after the score is forgotten.

This is the beauty of senior golf—and it is the reason golf is so enjoyable, at any age. If you hit one truly good shot in a round, no matter what you scored, that one shot will be enough to make your day. If you don't have this perspective, maybe you should.

"The senior tour has given me the chance to see old friends again and also meet some great golfers I've never played with. Recently, I was paired with Bobby Locke. It wouldn't have been a tragedy to go through life never having played with Locke, but still it was gratifying to have the experience. I can still see in the man a sparkle of those things that won him four British Opens.

"I remember one shot in particular during the first round of that tournament. We both had missed the fourth green. Our balls were a few feet apart in a swale in heavy grass with the pin cut close by. I had a perfect lie and he had a mediocre one. I'd have bet him $20 to $5 he couldn't get down in two; it was that difficult a shot. I myself took three to get down. Bobby just trickled his ball up there and the minute it hit

the green I knew it was going to be stone dead. It
went in the hole.

"One thing that makes senior golf so wonderful is
that the emphasis is on individuals, not scores. And
that is as it should be." — Paul Runyan

"We have golfers at our club in Houston who don't
hit the ball 150 yards, but they enjoy it. They say,
'I've got my game down from 32 to 30 since last
month.' No matter how badly you play, you can still
enjoy golf because you're on the most beautiful
playground of any sport." — Jimmy Demaret

Jimmy Demaret   Paul Runyan

Those two quotes represent the opposite ends of the spectrum in
golf. Never has the game known a more intense competitor than
Paul Runyan or a greater free spirit than Jimmy Demaret. Yet golf is
their common denominator, their antidote for despair, a source of
comfort and relaxation. Golf has been their friend for more than 60
years. It is my hope that this book will help make golf a better friend
to you as well.

2 REVIEWING THE BASICS OF YOUR SWING WITH THE GAME'S GRAND MASTER

Sam Snead has done for senior golf what Roger Bannister did for the four-minute mile. He broke a mental barrier. He raised our hopes and expectations. He proved anew we can grow old gracefully.

Sam Snead has played good golf not only longer than anyone else ever, but longer than anyone else ever thought possible. Who doubts that golf is the game of a lifetime when Sam's biological age usually approximates his average score?

Snead may be the greatest athlete of all time, but the secret to his longevity I think is not his athletic coordination. It is his supreme desire, his competitive spirit. I have never met anyone in my life who enjoys golf and delights in winning more than Sam Snead. You could say that Sam has played competitive golf every day of his life and not be far from the truth.

"It's like anything else. You don't lose it as fast if you keep at it. It's when you stop playing and then try to go back that you've lost it." — Sam Snead

Sam's "secret" is that he has never stopped and, as you will see in the accompanying photographs, he has never lost it. The comparison on the following pages shows Snead's swing in his first year on tour, 1937, at age 25, and his swing today, more than four decades later. In the early pictures, Sam weighed about 170 pounds and drove the ball 285-290 yards. Today, he admits to weighing 190 pounds but is probably closer to 200—although he has kept his body in wonderful shape—and drives the ball 250-260 yards.

I've tried in my analysis of Snead to relate his old swing to his modern swing, and then relate both of them to your swing. It is a tall order, but Sam serves as such a good example that my teaching and your learning should come as natural as, well, his playing.

To the untrained eye, nothing much has changed about Sam's swing. He still has that smooth, silken motion that for literally generations has made his swing the standard by which all others are measured. Actually, Snead has made some key adjustments over the years—many unconsciously, I'm sure—to accommodate the bodily changes of aging.

Although playing golf every day keeps his muscles strong and supple, Snead's backswing has shortened a bit as he's gotten older. It's only natural that you lose a few inches from your swing, but many senior golfers cut their backswings off at belt high and lose a few feet! Sam still makes a full swing that's comparable with many of the players on the PGA Tour who are young enough to be his grandchildren.

"If you're short when you're young, you'll never get it back when you're older. My backswing isn't as long as it used to be. I used to be able to swing back past horizontal, but now it's just short of parallel. I work pretty hard on keeping it long. The longer your backswing, the better chance you have for slowing down your tempo."—Sam Snead

Because he's about 25 or 30 pounds heavier than in his prime, Sam's swing nowadays takes longer from start to finish. A beefy guy moves slower than a skinny guy, right? So Sam allows himself more time to swing the club around his body, which is something the average senior can learn from. As you get older, your swing should get slower and remain as long as possible. You should do everything in your power to prevent it from getting shorter and faster.

Sam is the ultimate example for the senior golfer. While looking at the distinct stages of his swing on the following pages, remember the glue that holds them together is his slow, smooth tempo.

1. Pre-cock your head to promote full swing

The first thing I notice about Sam Snead's address position, today and 44 years ago, is that he cocks his head to the right before starting the swing. Sam says it helps him stay out of his own way. Pre-cocking the head to the right allows you to swing your arms farther around your body, turn your shoulders with less restriction and create the biggest arc possible, which is the basis for a lasting swing. Notice, also, the difference in Snead's grip positions. In the old photo, Sam's hands were turned to the right on the club, giving him what's called a "strong" grip. In the modern photo, he has a relatively "weak" grip, with the hands turned more to the left. I think the average golfer should use Snead's old grip, because it promotes greater hand and wrist action, which helps you draw the ball for more distance. If anything else has changed over the years, it may be that Snead's stance has narrowed slightly so that he can make an easier, fuller turn. With his right knee kicked in, as it is in both pictures, I'd say he's got 55 percent of his weight on the right leg. Setting up on the right puts you in position to shift to the left on the downswing. Snead's ball position appears to be off his right heel, but that is due to the camera angle. Actually, Snead has positioned the ball directly opposite his left heel in both sequences.

2. Start clubhead back along target line

*In both the old and new sequences, Snead starts
the club away from the ball with his hands, arms
and shoulders moving together. The difference is
that in the 1930s Sam almost immediately took the
club inside the target line and today he swings it
back more along the target line. This is due to the
change in grip positions. Sam's old "strong" grip
accentuated wrist action in the swing, so the
clubhead moved inside earlier on the takeaway and
the right hip turned away quicker. With the
modern "weak" grip, Snead's swing is controlled by
the forearms rather than by the wrists and hands,
which keeps the clubhead moving back on the
target line longer. While I recommend adopting
Snead's old grip, I think you should imitate his
modern takeaway. Start the clubhead back along
the target line and then let it move inside, rather
than snatching it abruptly inside at the start.*

3. Let the clubface open on the backswing

The critical difference between Snead's old and modern swings at this point is the position of the clubface. Today, his clubface swings open to the target line on the backswing, then returns to square at impact. This is a result of the natural rotation of Sam's arms swinging back and through. He is letting it happen without making any manipulations with his hands. Actually, he's keeping the clubface square to the swing plane throughout. This is another characteristic that makes his present swing the superior technical performance it is. In his old swing, the left wrist and hand moved back in one piece and held the clubface closed until the very top of the backswing. The longer you hold the clubface closed on the backswing, the more pressure it puts on your wrists and hands at the most critical stage of the swing—changing direction at the top. Snead used to be able to manipulate the clubface from closed to open at the top because of his tremendous strength and coordination. But he has developed a more consistent, repeating swing by using the whole length of the backswing to open the clubface.

4. Allow the left heel to come off the ground

More than 40 years older and 25 pounds heavier, Snead doesn't swing the club back quite as far as he used to. In the 1930s his clubshaft reached well past parallel at the top of his backswing, while today it's just short of parallel. The main reason, of course, is that he's gotten thicker through the upper torso and lost some suppleness. But unlike many golfers his age, he still makes a full enough swing because his upper body works in harmony with his lower body. It's as if they were tied together by rubber bands—the hands tied to the feet, the wrists tied to the ankles, the arms tied to the legs and the shoulders tied to the hips. As Snead swings the club to the top of the backswing, the rubber bands are stretched taut. Most graphically, the swinging of the left arm around his body pulls the left heel off the ground. In the old photo, Sam's arms swung farther around his body, pulling his left heel higher off the ground. In the modern photo, Snead's swing has shortened a bit, but the left heel still raises, allowing him to make a fuller swing. The simple act of lifting your left heel will help you lengthen your swing, transfer your weight and improve your tempo. It is a must for the senior golfer.

5. Start down by dropping the left heel

Snead triggers the change of direction by dropping his left heel to the ground, which drops his hands into position on the inside of the target line. The rubber bands, stretched taut at the top of the backswing, now snap to start the downswing. It then appears that his downswing is controlled through the hands, arms and shoulders, without much lower body drive. This motion is quite different from, say, that of Jack Nicklaus, who has a powerful leg drive and shifts faster to his left, with the lower body controlling the downswing. You may notice also that in Sam's old swing the left knee has already begun moving toward the target, which means he shifted his weight back to the left quicker when he was younger. Today he has to depend upon the speed of his upper body to create clubhead speed, with very little use of the legs as a supplementary force. In the old swing, he's flexing the knees and driving better with his lower body, which accounts for his greater distance in those days. You should feel your downswing starting from the ground up—the left heel drops and the legs, arms, hands, and clubhead move in a chain reaction.

6. Lead with the legs on the downswing

On the downswing, the left knee pulls and the right knee pushes, which Snead demonstrates beautifully in his old swing. His modern swing, however, shows a slight separation of leg action—the right knee lagging behind the left. He doesn't retain the angle of the club with the left arm moving down from the inside as well as he did in his younger days. A golf swing is a race to the ball that should be won by the legs, with the arms following and the hands catching up. Sam's hands are winning the race to the ball. To prevent a pull hook, he hangs on with his left arm, which causes him to fade the ball nowadays. The average golfer is not strong enough in his upper body to compensate as Sam does. You should learn to shift your weight from right to left on the downswing, moving your feet and legs and allowing the arms to follow and the hands to react.

7. Deliver clubhead at impact from inside

Observe the difference in Snead's grip at impact, old vs. new. In both cases, he appears to have returned to the same position as at address. In the old swing, the strong grip promoted an in-to-out swing path, resulting in a right-to-left shot pattern. In the old photo, his upper body was tilted more to the right, which indicates that he delivered the clubhead from the inside with a quick turn of the hips—thus, the violent action evident in the creases of his pants legs. In the modern swing, Snead turns his hips a little earlier in the downswing and then holds on with his left side, resulting in a cutting, or left-to-right, shot pattern. I wouldn't call it a blocking action, because he doesn't start the ball to the right of the target. It starts left and fades to the target. He hits the ball with a "contained blow" today, which explains his improved control. The average golfer probably needs distance more than control, so he should try to emulate Snead's old swing at impact, with the clubhead being delivered from the inside to draw the ball.

8. *Let your head come up on follow-through*

Here is another example of how Snead's swing has improved with age. He looks up on the shot after impact, which believe it or not is good. In the old photo, Sam held his head rigidly down, tilted slightly to the right and kept too much weight on the right side. This put pressure on his lower body, particularly at the base of his back. In the modern swing, Snead does what comes naturally—he allows his head to come up after impact and follow the flight of the ball. His left hip turns out of the way, his hands and arms cross over freely, and the through-swing is supported by the left leg. Remember, weight must follow motion. Transfer your weight from right to left on the through-swing and use your left leg as the support.

9. Finish in a relaxed position

I like Snead's follow-through in the modern swing, but I don't like it in the old sequence. Today his body "rides" better with the shot. We should all emulate his finish—practically all the weight on the left leg and just the right toe on the ground for balance. His follow-through exudes a sense of relaxation and ease. Again the upper body is working in harmony with the lower body. The "rubber band" tying his right hand to his right foot pulls the right heel off the ground on the follow-through. In the old photo, he finished in what's popularly called a reverse-C position, which I think is contrived and puts excess pressure on the back. Notice that more weight was being exerted on his right foot in the old photo, indicating that he's still hanging to the right on the finish. You can get away with that when you're young, but not when you get older. Nowadays Sam sometimes doesn't finish quite so high because he is afraid of hooking the ball and therefore cuts off the length of his swing. But when ol' Sam is hitting the ball well, there is still no better picture-postcard follow-through. It is classic, in the strictest sense of the word.

3 GETTING BETTER WITH AGE: 3 CARDINAL PRINCIPLES FOR ALL SENIORS

The premise for this book is that age is not the insurmountable barrier many of us think it is. As a senior golfer, you still can do anything you did 20, 30 or even 40 years ago, with three provisos:

1) You give your body enough time to do it, by slowing down your tempo and lengthening your swing.

2) You learn to draw the ball—curving it from right to left in flight—to obtain more distance for the same effort.

3) You keep your body in decent shape.

Let's look briefly at these three cardinal principles for all seniors before considering any specific adjustments in your setup and swing.

1. Slow Down Your Tempo and Lengthen Your Swing

You may have heard of the great English golf teacher, Ernest Jones, who demonstrated the golf swing by tying a penknife to a handkerchief, instructing his students to "swing the clubhead." Jones came over to this country and rose to prominence between the

Try to make a full swing — and you will

Senior golfers often tell me they can't turn enough to make a full swing. That's ridiculous in most cases. They simply don't try. Consider this venture: If you were standing erect and someone behind you called your name, your instinctive reaction would be to keep your feet in place and simply turn your head and shoulders to look at that person. With minimal effort, you probably would turn your shoulders 90 degrees, which is more than enough for a full swing in golf.

world wars, teaching at the Women's National Golf and Tennis Club in Glen Head, N.Y., and later at an indoor school in Manhattan. When a prospective student would call to arrange for lessons, Jones used to detail the most elaborate, round-about directions to his office. The student upon arrival usually asked why he was given such a tortuous route. "I wanted to see if you could follow instructions," Jones would say. The lesson had already begun.

The point of this story is that learning is an active, dynamic process, involving give and take, trial and error, questioning and understanding. For you to benefit from the instructions and ideas espoused in this book, you must be willing to work at them. Presumably Ernest Jones lost some pupils along the way with his convoluted directions, but as a result he taught only the people willing to listen and learn.

Ernest Jones comes to mind at this moment, also, because his definition of the golf swing is the Holy Grail for senior golfers. Jones defined the swing as "a measure of time that few people have learned to pace." It is a measure of time for the club to move from the address position at the ball, to the top of the backswing, down and through impact to a high follow-through at the finish. The secret of playing good golf lies in learning to pace this measure of time.

I firmly believe that there's nothing you cannot do at age 50 or 60 or 70 that you could do at 20 or 30 or 40; it just takes you longer to do it. That includes everything from golf to sex. If you keep your body in decent shape, there's nothing you can't do, provided you give yourself enough time. I don't believe our bodies deteriorate nearly as fast as many people think. If they did, we'd have an excuse for playing worse golf. But that's not true in most cases. If we keep our muscle tone relatively firm, exercise occasionally and lead an active life, then we'll possess more than enough elasticity in our bodies to create the motion necessary to swing a golf club.

However, as we grow older, our muscles tend to react slower. Therefore, we need to give them more time to react. This applies to everything we do. We should give ourselves more time to sleep the night before a big match, more time to wake up and get ready in the morning, more time to eat breakfast, more time to drive to the course, more time to walk from the parking lot to the clubhouse, more time to hit practice balls and, most important of all, more time to swing the club. The idea is to slow down the tempo of your swing as well as the tempo of your life.

 *"I don't think one's tempo gets slower. If anything, it tries to speed up. I try to keep mine as slow as I can but it is still not as slow as I would like it or as it used to be. Somebody told me one time that he never knew any golfer that came on the PGA Tour whose swing tempo got slower. So when you see some young kid come on tour with a fast backswing, you know it is only going to get faster; it is not going to get slower."—Dan Sikes*

Part of the challenge of golf is controlling your tempo. The better you play and the more good shots you hit, the more you tend to quicken the pace. The good player learns to increase his swing speed only to a point that he can control. It's the challenge you face every time you play. You want to hit it as far as you can, but still keep it in the fairway. When you go beyond your limitations, you make bad shots. But half the fun is testing your limits.

"I drive the ball more consistently now than I ever did, but I don't hit it nearly as far. If all I try to do is hit it straight, I can gear myself to do that. In fact, sometimes now I hit it so straight it's almost . . . well, I hate to use the word, but it's almost boring. I'd really like to hit it longer. But when I try for more distance, I'm presented with other problems. Like finding the ball."—Arnold Palmer

When Jack Nicklaus needs to hit the ball farther on those occasions when more distance is required, he says he concentrates on taking it back slower. That should be the credo of the senior golfer. Otherwise, if you're fast going back, you must be doubly fast coming through; your sense of timing and body awareness must be keen and alert to maintain that clubhead speed.

"I'll never forget what Sam Snead once told me about my fast backswing. He compared hitting a golf ball with hitting a nail with a hammer. The harder you hit the nail, the slower you take the hammer back. Same thing in golf.

"I try to copy Snead's swing, specifically by avoiding too hasty a takeaway, by getting some rhythm going in my feet, and by achieving as wide an arc as I can, with my hands high. I'm of the old school: I try for a good, wide hip turn."—Bill Campbell

What is the surest way to slow down your tempo? Simply, it is to take a bigger swing. All golf's great players whose games have endured possessed long, fluid swings, allowing themselves more time to develop clubhead speed and momentum to hit the ball consistently. That's why good players, as they get older, continue to keep their swings long. But many senior amateurs—and some pros—have allowed age to shorten their swings, which gives the muscles less time to react and decreases the margin of error.

"Many years ago, I looked at the people I was teaching—45 and 50 years of age with short backswings—and I promised myself that when I got to be 45 or 50 or 70, I was going to have a full swing. And I have worked on that for a long time, and I think to a certain degree I've succeeded. If there's one thing I've learned about golf after years of hard study, it is that a long swing will outlast a short swing every time."—George Fazio

George Fazio obviously made up his mind to keep his swing long and did it, which goes to show what you can do with determination.

Unless you have a bad back or some other ailment, you can make almost any adjustment you really want to.

Golf is a nonviolent game played violently from within. You can make as violent or as nonviolent a swing at the ball as you like. You can swing as long or as short as you want. But it's entirely up to you. Your destiny lies in your hands.

"My swing hasn't shortened at all over the years. You will find that as you get older, if you keep your swing long, you'll maintain your distance off the tee a heck of a lot better. So I've tried to keep my swing as long as possible."—George Bayer

"Don't ever worry about over-swinging. Look at January. He swings the club well past parallel and he still plays beautifully. I played with him when he was a kid at North Texas State and today at age 51 he still swings the same way."—Mike Souchak

"I remember exactly how I developed a long swing as a kid. No one taught it to me; it just happened. My parents were country people living in the city. We spent the summer when I was 12 or 13 back in the country visiting with some kin folk. When I left Dallas, the kids I was playing golf with at Stevens Park were hitting the ball the same distance as me. But when I came back they all had grown and they were outdriving me 40 yards. I was getting my brains beat out and I wasn't going to stand for that. So I grabbed the practice sack and worked until I found a way to hit it farther. I just learned to rear back and hit it hard enough to stay out there with the other kids."—Don January

January's swing may be even longer now and certainly his tempo is slower, which gives him more time to change direction and control the forward action of his swing. His backswing around his upper body is slower, allowing him to get in position with his lower body to start the clubhead down. Which makes him as good a player now as he ever was.

"I think we all swing too fast off the ball. You have to be nice and slow and deliberate, then progressively pick up the tempo. I have seen good players go slow-fast and I've seen good players go slow-slow. Never have I seen a good player go fast starting anything. Fast will not get it. Fast-slow won't get it either. Once you put fast first, you're a dead turkey."—Don January

Doug Ford, on the other hand, is an example of a relatively short, fast swinger, so it's been more difficult for him to maintain his game. He won't be able to develop as much clubhead speed as he gets older and he'll have more off-center hits. So he's not going to be as consistent now as he was 20 years ago. Fortunately for Doug, he's one of the game's all-time great competitors. Knowing him, he'll find a way to get the ball out there and in the hole in one less stroke than the next guy, but it won't be easy.

"I have always been a short swinger. Not that I think it is a good thing—the seniors who play the best are the ones who have retained their full backswings. I am basically a hands player, but to play that way requires a lot of practice. I have gotten a little bit longer by practicing more of a turn away from the ball, which gives me more time to develop clubhead speed."—Doug Ford

Gardner Dickinson and Dan Sikes, who play as partners in the Legends of Golf, also are firm believers in making as full a swing as possible. And the proof is in the pudding, because they are two of the longest drivers among the senior players.

"If I could give one bit of advice to the average senior it would be: Turn till you can't turn any more, and then turn some more. It's critical that every golfer develops a full swing and keeps working at maintaining that length."—Gard-ner Dickinson

"Never try to shorten your swing, because it's going to shorten up with time, anyway. I've never known anybody whose swing got longer as he got older. If you learn to play golf with a nice full swing, you're probably going to be a better senior player than the fellow who has a three-quarter swing when he's young.

"I feel I hit the ball almost as far, and sometimes I get to driving as far, as I ever did. Certainly I'm one of the longest of the guys who play the senior tour, and I attribute that to the fact that I have a big shoulder turn. The reason I developed a big shoulder turn was because I wanted to maximize the feeling that I was hitting the ball with my body rather than with my hands. At the height of my career, when I was playing my best, my basic thought was to make a big turn. As I've gotten older, it has become harder to turn that much. It's not impossible, but it requires more practice."—Dan Sikes

Obviously, tempo and swing length are vital factors of longevity in golf. Many senior pros consider them to be the foremost areas of improvement for the average senior. But lest the discussion be taken too seriously, I'm reminded of a story told by Ralph Guldahl, the U.S. Open champion in 1937 and '38:

"When I was a kid, and thin as a beanpole, I used to take the club back way past horizontal. Now as hard as I try, it only goes back about three-quarters. An old Scotsman once told me, 'Ralph, I've seen all you young guys come along with long backswings and as the years go by the swings get shorter and shorter, until eventually you have no backswings at all!'

"I remember when Jock Hutchison and Freddie McLeod, who were both well into their 80s, used to lead off the parade at the Masters. They only swung back to about belt high. So now I think to myself that I should live so long that I only swing back to belt high." — Ralph Guldahl

2. Learn to draw the ball for more distance

To hook or slice, that is the question. If you observe the game's best players—Jack Nicklaus, Tom Watson and Lee Trevino, all of whom prefer to work the ball left to right—you would probably conclude that the ideal shot pattern is a fade. As a matter of fact, the average golfer (particularly the senior) should learn to draw the ball, because a right-to-left shot is longer in both carry and overall distance than a left-to-right shot. This conclusion is based on (1) my years of experience as a player and teacher, and (2) machine tests conducted by *Golf Digest* at the Titleist facilities in New Bedford, Mass., and by the United States Golf Association at its range in Far Hills, N.J.

The testing by *Golf Digest* was done on a True Temper swing machine set at 90 miles per hour—about average for a good amateur player—with the driver clubface turned 1½ degrees closed for a draw and 1½ degrees open for a fade. Following is a report published by the magazine:

> Into a slight headwind, the drawn shots averaged 233 yards in carry and roll, the fades only 216. They finished an average of 18 yards to the left or right of center.
>
> The lower-flying draws rolled farther than the higher-soaring fades, 16 or 17 yards compared with less than nine—because the landing angle was less severe. But the draws also carried farther, an average of 217 yards for the draw and less than 208 for the fade.
>
> Frank Thomas, the USGA's technical director, explains it simply: when the clubface is open to the swing path at impact, loft is added to the club, the ball is launched at a higher angle, more backspin is added and the aerodynamic effects of "lift" and "drag" on the ball in flight are increased. At the same time, the forward speed generally is decreased. So the ball sails higher, tailing to the right because of the initial clockwise spin imparted by the open clubface, but it does not go as far.

As the illustration shows, the higher-flying fade does not carry as far as the lower drawn shot. The fade also does not roll nearly as far because of its steeper landing angle. The result is a dramatic loss of distance

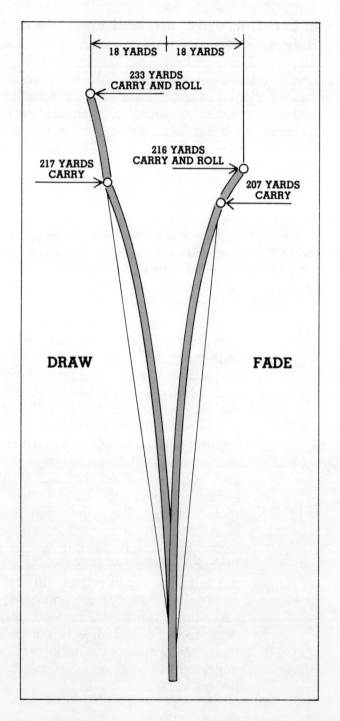

When the face is closed at impact, the opposite happens. The loft of the club and the launch angle of the ball are decreased, less backspin is created and forward speed is increased. The ball flies lower and, because of the counterclockwise spin created at impact, curves to the left. While backspin is necessary to keep the ball in the air, apparently the effect of less backspin is more than offset by the increase in forward speed, so the ball carries farther.

It seems extremely critical to me, then, that as a golfer grows older and distance is a bigger obstacle, drawing the ball (right to left) becomes almost a necessity. Remember, these tests were conducted on machines with the swing path and angle of approach remaining constant. When a person hooks or slices, the swing path and angle usually change, too, so the differences may be even greater. Most senior golfers cannot afford to give up 15 or 20 yards per tee shot. If a need for greater distance is highest on your priority list, learn to draw the ball. I'll give you specific swing thoughts and set-up keys as we go along. For now, I'd just like you to realize that the draw is your optimum shot pattern.

"As I've gotten older, I've gone from being a slicer to being a hooker. I made the change to get a little more distance. I thought the courses were getting longer, or maybe I was just getting shorter.

"Drawing the ball definitely is better for the average player, especially the senior. To hit it right to left, you usually make a bigger turn and swing the clubhead through impact more from the inside-out, which puts you in a more powerful position. It gives you leverage to create more clubhead speed."—Dow Finsterwald

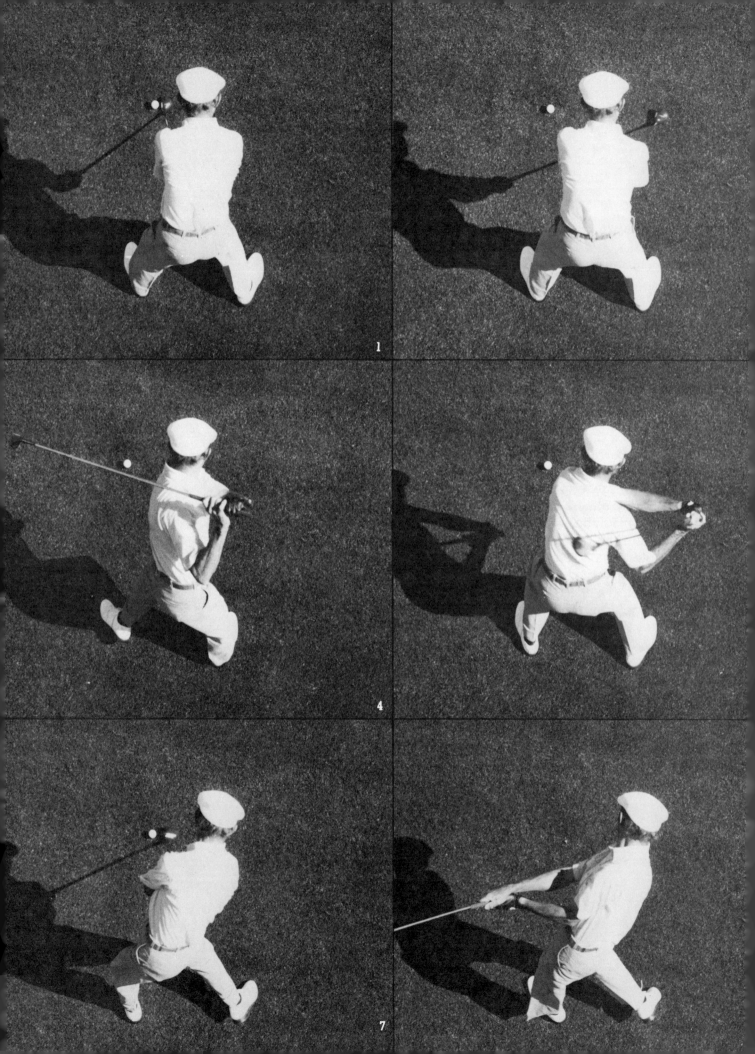

The head moves, the legs support

Rigidness is the No. 1 enemy of the senior player. The body must move freely and easily throughout the swing, if you are to develop a full, unrestricted motion. This sequence demonstrates that the head moves noticeably on the backswing. It also illustrates how the legs are used to support the swinging of the arms.

Notice that the ball is just outside my left ear at address. As the club swings back, my head obviously moves several inches to the right. Now study how my legs drive and my shoulders turn to the left on the forward swing. But does my head move to the left? Hell, no! My head actually moves farther to the right and stays behind the ball so I hit forward and upward with the driver. This angle of approach gives me more power and distance. The point is it's no big deal if your head moves to the right on the backswing, provided it doesn't move to the left on the forward swing. In fact, if your head remains locked at address, it'll stifle your swing and probably cause a reverse pivot.

Next, observe my address position, which I recommend for most senior players. The stance is closed, my shoulders and hips are square to the target line, I am bending at the hips, and my head extends in front of my knees and feet.

Notice also that I coil around my right leg for support on the backswing and then move against my left leg to support my forward swing. These photographs graphically demonstrate the use of my legs as supports for the swinging of my arms.

Build left side strength

Try this isometric exercise to develop strength in your left hand, wrist, arm and shoulder. Holding the club with only your left hand, make a backswing and hold your position at the top. Count to 10. Then swing the club half way down so your arm is in the 9 o'clock position and count to 10 again. Then bring the club down to impact and hold it there, again counting to 10. When you begin to do this exercise with ease, extend the number you count to—next try 20, then 30, etc.

Develop your muscle flexibility

Here's a morning wake-me-up exercise that also will help develop muscle suppleness. Without a club, swing your right arm alone to the top-of-the-backswing position and hold it there for a few seconds. Then swing down and follow through making as full an extension as possible, and hold. Repeat and alternate the exercise with your left arm.

3. Exercise to Keep Your Muscles Young

I must confess right off that I don't do a regular regimen of exercises, but I lead a physically active life. I'm teaching on a range every day, constantly on my feet, walking and running up and down the line. I'm bending and stooping to tee up balls for students. I'm demonstrating the swing all the time. And at the end of the day, I often hit balls or go out to play a quick nine holes. I also swim and do some forms of structured exercise occasionally. Consequently, my muscles—the ones used in the golf swing especially—are strong and flexible.

The senior golfer tends to lose the strength and suppleness of his muscles as he gets older because he doesn't stay physically active. If you feel you're losing distance because of a lack of muscle resiliency, check with your doctor before starting any exercise program.

I've always felt that the best exercise for the golfer is to swing a weighted club. Jerry Barber, one of my fellow senior professionals, in my opinion makes the finest exercise club. It weighs about 32 ounces, or two and a half times the weight of a regular driver. There are other heavy clubs or weighted rings that you could use; most pro shops sell them. You could even swing a couple of irons at once. Swing as you would normally, feeling your muscles stretch as they extend on the backswing and on the follow-through. Make an exaggerated weight shift—to the right and then to the left—allowing your feet to come off the ground, as if striding back and forth like a batter in baseball.

Another good exercise for developing suppleness is to assume an address position without a club and swing your left arm around your body as far as you can, turning your back to the "target," and hold it there a few seconds; then swing your right arm around your body as far as you can, facing your stomach to the "target," and hold it there for a few more seconds. Do this several times in the morning and at night before you go to bed. It's also a good first-tee warm-up exercise if you don't have time to hit balls.

Isometric exercises are good for developing strength. In my clinics I sometimes challenge my students to a contest of holding the club in position at the top of the backswing with just the left hand. Most people's arms sag after only a few seconds, but I can hold it up there for several minutes. Try it and you'll be surprised how heavy a 13-ounce club can feel. I even recommend it as a form of isometric

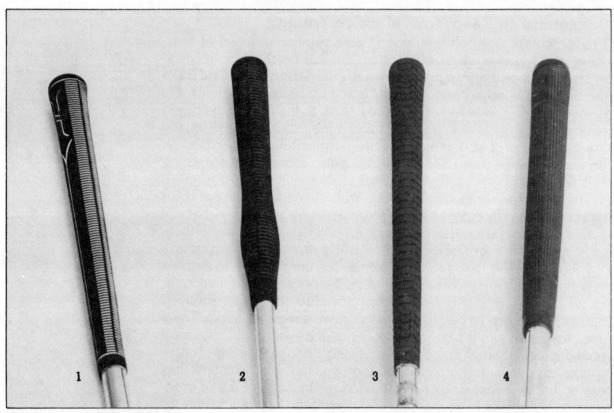

Grips for arthritis sufferers

Here's a sampling of grips designed for golfers with arthritis in their hands. Most are made of a softer rubber with diameters larger than standard. The bigger the grip, the easier it is for the hands to hold on, which is very good for arthritic golfers. The problem you have with a big grip is that it puts more weight in the handle and may throw off the balance of the club. When installing heavier grips, have your pro retain the swing weight of each club.

1. Arthritic grip, *by Eaton/Golf Pride—soft, molded rubber/cork compound designed to absorb shock of impact.*

2. Hourglass grip, *by Eaton/Golf Pride—hourglass shape found easier to hold by arthritis sufferers.*

3. Chamois grip, *by Avon—resilient, soft rubber grip designed with "air chambers to cushion shock of improperly hit shots."*

4. Sensation grip, *by Tacki-Mac—one-eighth inch oversize grip made of tacky material called Kraton, with special serrated surface for better traction and easier gripping.*

exercise to strengthen your left side.

A waggle is another form of exercise that you can practice anywhere. Just set up to an imaginary ball and waggle the club head back and forth for a couple of minutes. It's a great developer of wrist, hand and finger strength.

Finally, one last exercise that you can do at home or at the office is simply to grip and regrip a club. Some teachers advocate squeezing a rubber ball to strengthen the hands and fingers, but I think the best device is an old club, preferably one that has an over-size grip and is weighted extra heavy. Keep it near your desk for those extended telephone conversations with gabby business associates.

But let's not kid ourselves that a few minutes of exercise a day will rid us of all the problems of aging. Our eyesight, particularly depth perception to the target, tends to get poorer as we get older, so we need to rely more on yardage in club selection. Although I'm certainly not afflicted, many seniors tend to gain weight, usually in the centers of their bodies, which puts a greater stress on the legs to support the turning of the trunk. Gaining weight may change a person's posture, make him rotate more around his body in the swing, putting more stress on his hands and wrists. And perhaps the most serious aging problem for the golfer is arthritis. Fortunately, today manufacturers are experimenting with different grip materials and shapes to ease the pain of arthritis in a golfer's hands, but even a redesigned grip cannot alleviate the problem in other parts of the body.

"Arthritis has just about destroyed my golf game. I play very little now. I'm a high 70s, low 80s shooter. I have a tough time breaking 40 each nine. If I can break 40 for nine, at 69 years of age, I can enjoy that and be happy with it. But I can't enjoy shooting in the 80s.

"I have arthritis in my wrists and the middle part of my back, where there are arthritis spurs, so to speak, or calcium deposits that extend around to my right front ribs. When I stay down and through the swing, it puts pressure on my right side and that hurts. So I come off the ball a lot and raise up. I don't stay down and under and through the way I used to,

and the net result is that I play poorly. I've learned to live with the arthritis in my wrists and in my left knee pretty well. That's not hurt my golf nearly like the condition in the right side, because that's the side that has to stay under the shot." — Byron Nelson

Nelson's particular form of arthritis—in the lower ribs of the right side—obviously makes swinging a club a difficult and painful chore, yet he's capable of hitting wonderful shots when he puts his mind to it. Nelson and I staged a clinic in Toledo ahead of the 1979 U.S. Open at Inverness, and I remember him saying he wasn't going to hit any full shots. I introduced him as the greatest striker of the golf ball that ever lived and went on to say: "No one in history has ever hit a driver off the fairway like this man. He was the best. Now I wouldn't dare ask him to come out here and hit balls off the fairway with his driver because he has some physical problems that he never had when he was a great player." Byron jumped off the fence, ran out there and began hitting some of the damndest shots I'd ever seen. He was whipping the driver off the ground like there was nothing to it—and that is the toughest shot in golf, bar none. Here was a guy under stress and pain, to some degree, and in 15 minutes he relived his whole golf game. It just goes to show what inspiration can do. I've always been impressed with Byron as a player and a man. What most impresses me is how unimpressed he is with himself. He never tries to show any authority, and he has a beautiful, unassuming way of handling people. It's too bad he cannot play competitively now.

4 8 CHECKPOINTS TO REJUVENATE YOUR SETUP AND SWING

The first warning sign of a golf swing that's getting old in a hurry is loss of distance off the tee. If you don't take measures to halt this backward slide as soon as it starts, it will spread like wildfire to the rest of your game. Because you're not hitting it as far off the tee, you'll be using a little more club and swinging harder on your approach shots, so your chance for error will be greater and you'll miss more greens. Then a bigger strain will be put on your short game. You'll find yourself playing more sand shots, pitches, chips and long putts. The more three- and four-foot saving putts you're faced with, the more you inevitably will miss. So you begin to doubt your short game and wonder if you have the yips. By that time, your whole game is infected and you're swinging like an old man. What you need to do is step back and take a fresh look at your approach to the game. In this chapter are eight checkpoints to keep your swing young. Each is a two-minute refresher course on a specific aspect of the setup or swing that I have found to be particularly valuable for senior golfers. The most effective way to apply these checkpoints to your game is to practice them one at a time. When you're hitting practice balls, concentrate on just one of the swing thoughts described here. Work on them individually until they become a natural part of your whole routine.

1. Modernize Your Grip

The most startling change in the golf swing in the last 30 years has to do with the placement of the left hand on the club. When I learned the game, we were taught to hold the club in the fingers and then close the palm over the grip. This strengthened the left hand on the club—pointing the V formed by the base of the thumb and forefinger toward the right shoulder—and prompted excessive wrist action in the swing. The first glimpse I got of the modern grip was in watching Ben Hogan practice. Face on at address, I could see that the back of his left hand pointed squarely at the target and only one or two knuckles were apparent (instead of the normal three or four knuckles). And from behind at address, I noticed the manner in which he regripped the club with his left hand—his last three fingers opened and closed against his palm, indicating to me he was holding the club more in the palm of his hand than the fingers. This grip was a revelation. It allowed Hogan to rotate his forearms and use his legs to support his arm swing and stabilize the force of the clubhead through the ball. The old grip promoted a loose, flailing, wristy swing that emphasized the role of the hands and hips. The modern grip promoted greater control, distributed better the workload of all the muscles in the swing and produced more of an arm-and-leg action.

The modern grip is based on the principle that the hands must work together. For the hands to work in unison, the palms must face one another on the grip. I think the senior player ought to play with a grip turned slightly to the right in what's called a stronger position, but not turned drastically to the right as in the old grip. The modern position puts the left arm in a dominant role at address, making it higher and the right arm lower, which is conducive to drawing the ball. It gives the player the ability to turn the club around his body, get the path on the inside of the target line and rotate the forearms to strike through the ball.

As far as the right hand is concerned, I like to see it snugly placed against the left, with the palm facing squarely against the left. The closer the hands are together on the club, the better they can work together—so for that reason, I recommend the overlapping or interlocking grip. But that's not to say that other players haven't succeeded with other, more unorthodox grips. Art Wall and Bob Rosburg, for instance, have always used the baseball grip, with all ten fingers

Outdated Grip
The old grip taught when I learned the game had the left hand on the club in a very strong position with the palm facing toward the ground and three or four knuckles apparent to the golfer. The club was held in the fingers and the palm turned over the grip. This formed almost a right angle between the left forearm and hand. Golfers with this grip tend to have a loose swing and flail at the ball, often producing duck-hooks and little control.

Modern Grip

*The modern grip has the palms facing each other
on the club. For the senior golfer, I recommend
turning the hands slightly to the right so the V's
formed by the thumbs and forefingers point
between the right eye and shoulder. This puts the
wrists in an elongated position at address
which prevents the swing from getting too loose or
wristy. I like to tell my students to "thimble" the
right thumb and forefinger. Compare your grip
with these pictures.*

on the club. They have succeeded in my opinion despite their grips, because they're very talented athletes.

"I've always played with a baseball grip. I started golf when I was two years old. My hands were so small I couldn't hold the club very well so I grabbed it with all the fingers I could. I tried interlocking for about three or four months in college, but I never stuck with it. I never had a lot of strength in my hands. You know those grip machines? I can't budge them off the mark.

"The position of my hands on the club is a bit unorthodox, too. My right hand is probably a hook grip and my left hand a fade grip. I try to feel my left hand 'catching' my right hand through the ball. I think I've had to fight a hook a little more as I've gotten older because my legs aren't moving as quickly as they used to."—Bob Rosburg

"I use the baseball grip because I didn't know there was any other way of holding the club when I started the game. Years ago, Tommy Armour suggested that I change my grip. I tried overlapping for about three days—I'm sure I didn't give it a good try—and went back to my old grip. It's just the most comfortable way for me to play."—Art Wall

2. Keep Grip Pressure Dynamic

Julius Boros has the strongest but yet softest, most supple hands I've ever seen. He reminds me of the story of the woman who wanted a strong man with a light touch, not a weak man with a heavy touch. Julius puts his hands on the club as if he were molding putty—slowly and softly. In fact, that's the way you should think of gripping the club. Start with a soft, putty-like grip, then mold it and let it firm up. Many senior players, trying to get more distance, hold the club tighter. Actually, this excess pressure limits their flexibility. A golfer with light grip pressure, like Boros, allows his wrists and arms to turn freely in a fuller swing.

Take a moment and participate in an experiment for me. Place your hands in the praying position, with palm facing palm, and push them together as hard as you can. Now try to move your arms back and forth. What happens to your arm motion? It feels very restricted, right? Well, that's what happens in the golf swing when you grip the club tightly. Now lighten the pressure in your hands and see how easily the arms move. I think most golfers confuse the term "firm" with "tight." It's all right to grip the club firmly, but you're flirting with disaster if you grip it too tightly.

"The best thing I've done to improve my game is holding onto the club with an easier effort. I concentrate on holding the club with lighter grip pressure now than ever before. I don't try to hit the ball as hard; I try to stay within myself. It's improved my timing and made a big change in my whole approach to the game. I used to grip the club tightly with all systems on 'go.' Everything was wide open and I really tried to rip it hard. That's when you lose your balance, your tempo—everything."—George Bayer

Don't take this to mean that you should always grip the club as lightly as you can. Grip pressure should be dynamic. It changes depending on the length and type of shot you're trying to play. Grip pressure on a putt is not going to feel like that on a drive. The momentum of the club swinging around your body to propel the ball farther with a longer club instinctively will make you hold the club with more pressure—and that's correct. When putting on a heavy green, for instance, your instinctive reaction will be to hold the club more firmly to hit the ball harder. When putting on a fast green, you'll naturally grip the club lighter.

Not only does grip pressure change depending on the type of shot you're playing, it changes during the course of the swing on every shot. Grip pressure gradually increases on the backswing and downswing, then dissipates through impact. The feeling is similar to that of a pitcher as he winds up and throws a baseball. He holds the ball with just enough pressure to control it. If he holds it too tightly, he won't release it properly. The pressure increases gradually as he winds up, but the moment the ball is released the pressure is gone.

My students often ask me the question, "Where do you feel pressure in your grip?" I agree with Byron Nelson who says that all parts of the hand feel pressure to one degree or another. You can't take the pressure out of one hand or one part of either hand.

Here's a more important question: Where do you feel the greatest pressure in your hands at the top of the backswing? If your answer is in the last three fingers of the left hand, you probably haven't completed your backswing. Ideally, the greatest pressure should be felt on the left thumb. At the top of the backswing, the shaft rests on the left thumb, and then as the forward swing begins, greater pressure to the thumb is applied as the left arm swings down and the shaft remains "loaded." The longer you feel this pressure on the thumb, the longer you've retained the angle. This gives you what's called "late release" and maximum distance.

Fluctuating Grip Pressure

Grip pressure in the swing is dynamic. It gradually increases as the club is swung around the body and then dissipates through impact. The grip pressure felt by a golfer is similar to that of a baseball pitcher. He holds the ball just lightly enough to control it. As he winds up, the pressure gradually increases. Then at the moment the ball is released, the pressure dissipates. For this reason, it's better to start with a light grip and gradually increase to a firm grip rather than going from firm to light, which restricts the freedom of your arm motion. Notice the flexibility and freedom of motion exhibited by this fine, young specimen of a baseball hurler.

Grip Pressure At the Top

The greatest pressure at the top of the backswing should be felt on the left thumb as the club shaft rests against it. As the forward swing begins and the arms pull down, the shaft lags behind still pressuring the left thumb. The longer this pressure is felt on the thumb, the longer the angle is retained. These pictures dramatically show the shaft pressing against the thumb on the forward swing. As the club is released and the wrists snap through impact, the pressure dissipates.

3. Set Arms in Position to Rotate

"You've got to play with the equipment you have. If you're a little heavy through the chest, it may be difficult to swing loose, but try. Take the biggest swing possible. And above all, loosen up your arms as much as you can. Only if your arms are soft and supple will you be able to make the turn necessary to hit the ball any distance."—Jay Hebert

I can't believe how many people play golf with elbows locked and wonder why they have tendinitis. Try walking with your arms straight at your sides and you'll feel like the Frankenstein monster. So why try to play golf that way? When you walk, your arms swing freely and bend easily at the elbows. It's not necessary to keep them perfectly straight. It's even more critical not to do it when you swing the club!

Think of using a scythe. The arms are in a relaxed position and the elbows fold with ease as the implement is swung back and forth. Keep your arms rigid and you won't cut much grass. Like a golf club, you have to swing the scythe around and away from your body.

At address I'd like to see the senior golfer play with the arms in a slightly bent position, despite what you may hear about keeping the left arm straight. This relaxed position helps you make a fuller turn and swing the club in a bigger arc for greater distance. The left arm will straighten automatically on the downswing once you learn to use your lower body correctly.

Swing with right arm only

An excellent drill to learn the feeling of how the arms work in the swing is to take one of the arms out of the swing. By that I mean, make a normal pass at the ball with only one hand on the club and the other in your pocket. Try it first with just your right arm swinging. Keep your arm relaxed, free of tension, and feel the clubhead lagging behind and then catching up through impact. This exercise helps you learn the proper way to bend the wrist and fold the elbow of the right arm as you swing back and move forward through the ball.

Swing with left arm only

*Now swing with your left arm alone on the club.
This exercise develops strength and control in your
left side. Practice hitting balls with both drills using
a short iron. Golf is a two-sided game, and these
drills help you learn the sequence of using your left
and right sides in the swing.*

4. Assume an Athletic Posture

Setting up to hit a golf ball should be as easy as leaning over to pick a flower, but it's not for most senior players because they've fallen into some bad habits. Let's try to purge our minds of all prior thoughts on posture and start over fresh.

Stand up and extend your arms by reaching out with your hands together and bend from the hips. Your weight will naturally fall toward the balls of your feet, as it does in practically every other athletic endeavor. The final step is to flex your knees slightly, so they are just over the laces of your shoes. Put a club in your hand and you've assumed the ideal position from which to hit a ball.

Tap your heels

To assume the proper athletic posture at address, put your hands together and extend them in front of you (A). Bend from the hips and flex slightly at the knees. Your weight automatically should fall toward the balls of your feet. Try rocking back and forth from heel to toe to feel this weight distribution. Put a club in your hand and you're *now ready to swing away (B). One final test I recommend to make sure your weight sets properly at address is to move your heels alternately in an up-and-down tapping motion. If you have to lift your head as you tap, your weight is too much on the heels. If the head stays relatively steady, your weight is on the balls of your feet.*

Don't just "sit"

Many senior golfers have been taught to "sit down to the ball." As a result, they don't bend from the hips sufficiently and flex at the knees too much in an effort to reach the ball. This creates undue pressure on the legs and at the base of the back. It hurts. Set up properly, bending from the hips and flexing slightly at the knees, you feel no pressure; your weight is supported by your legs, which allows you to turn and swing your arms around your body with ease.

A gauge to check your knee flex

The tendency of most senior players is to bend too much at the knees and not enough at the hips. Here's a simple gauge to check your knee flex at address. Place a club across your knee line as I've demonstrated here. Your knees should not be so straight that this line is inside your shoe laces (A). Also, your knees shouldn't be so flexed that this line is outside your toes, making your weight fall back toward your heels (B). Ideally, you should have about three or four inches of knee flex and your knee line should be just over your shoe laces (C).

5. Align Body for a Draw

The main problem with alignment is that people don't pay enough attention to it. They are careless about the way they aim the clubface and align their body to the target. Any senior golfer who plays from an open stance no doubt is costing himself yards off the tee. If you accept the notion that senior players should learn to draw or hook the ball, your alignment is fairly simple: Set up with your eyes, shoulders, hips and knees parallel with the target line, and your stance slightly closed or pointing to the right of the target. This puts you in the optimum position to turn the right side out of the way and coil around the right leg on the backswing, allowing you to turn fully with the least resistance.

Use 3 spare clubs to check alignment

Walk on to any practice range at a tour site and you'll find the top professionals practicing with clubs on the ground to check their alignment. I like to use three clubs—one just outside the target line to align the clubface square to the target, another parallel with the target line at my feet to make sure my stance is slightly closed, and a third parallel club just a few inches outside my feet to check my eyeline. These photographs illustrate in my opinion the ideal alignment for the senior player—eyes, shoulders, hips and knees parallel with the target line, and feet slightly closed.

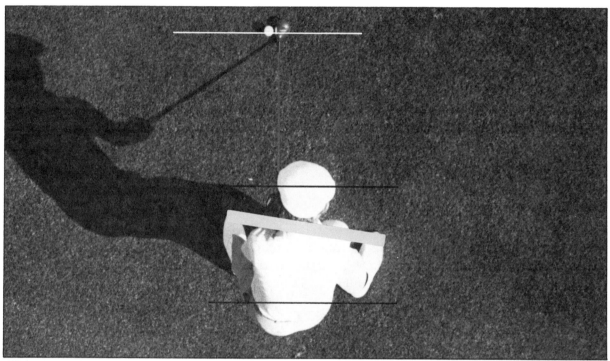

Alignment from above

This unusual view of my alignment at address from directly above again shows the fundamentals of a good senior setup. My eyes, shoulders and hips are parallel with the target line, and my feet are aligned slightly to the right of the target.

6. Start with Weight Right

Weight distribution is one of the simplest things in golf to understand, so why do so few people understand it? The reason obviously is because there are so many differences of opinion. My philosophy is pretty basic, though, and I think it's the best for the senior player. If you stood with your weight evenly distributed and put your hands together in a praying position and bent at the hips and flexed at the knees, your weight would remain evenly distributed. Now if you were to lower your right hand as you would in taking your grip, the weight naturally would go to your right side. That basically is why I think it's natural to start out with your weight on your right side at address.

Most people agree that the flow of weight should be toward the right side on the backswing and then back toward the left side on the forward swing. All this has to happen in the second and a half it takes to swing a club, so why not save a step. A senior player needs to allow himself more time to swing the club. If you set up on the right side at address, it gives you a head start for moving to your left leg on the forward swing.

Tommy Armour used to teach setting up on the left side, which I think is a mistake. Armour may have been able to set up left, but he was one of the game's all-time great "hands" players. His arms were like a gorilla's and his hands like meat hooks. By sheer strength he could drive the club through the ball with his weight on the left side, but that's not the approach most senior players can afford to take.

I think all full shots should be played with the weight predominantly on the right side. I'd say 60-40 for the driver, a slightly lesser ratio for the irons and just better than 50-50 for the wedge. The only time I'd recommend setting up left is on a short pitch or chip, where instead of looking for distance you want to strike down on the ball.

One excellent method to settle your weight at address is to waggle the club and at the same time rock back and forth, from right to left. Al Balding, the Canadian senior pro, is a fine example of a player who uses a waggle as part of his routine to trigger the swing.

Think of throwing a football

The weight shift in a golf swing is similar to the motion in most other sports. In football, for example, you throw a pass by shifting your weight to your right side, coiling onto your right leg. Then you change directions and move to your left leg, shifting your weight back again to the left. The principle is the same in golf. Because the golf swing takes only a second and a half from start to finish, I recommend starting with the weight predominantly on the right side to give senior players more time to shift to the left for maximum power.

7. Cock the Head at the Start

Almost every player throughout history cocked his head to the right at the start of the backswing. Harry Vardon, Bobby Jones, Sam Snead, Ben Hogan, Jack Nicklaus, Tom Watson—they all cock or cocked their head. Most of them did it as they started the backswing. Nicklaus, most pronouncedly, does it before starting the club back. The simple fact that all great golfers cock their heads would make me want to try it, but there's even a more powerful reason you should adopt the routine. All these players I mentioned—from Vardon to Watson—have or had terrific extension on the backswing. They all hit the ball a long way. Cocking your head to the right helps you swing the club back on the inside of the target line and return it there on the forward swing. It's one of the simplest adjustments you can make in your setup and it will help you create a bigger arc and smite the ball a longer distance.

"You can overdo that 'head-still' business and freeze your neck muscles and cut off your backswing. I like to swivel my head a little bit to the right as I start to swing the club back. It helps me make a free, full body turn. I'd recommend it especially to short or heavy-set golfers who have a hard time turning. It's a simple device to let you get out of your own way."
—Sam Snead

Pre-cock your head at address

*Most good players set up with their heads in a 12
o'clock position. Then just before taking the club
back or at the start of the backswing, they swivel or
cock their heads to 1 o'clock. To adopt this routine,
begin by looking at the ball out of your left eye.
This head position allows you to make a fuller
shoulder turn and reach maximum extension on the
backswing. Locking your head rigidly at 12 o'clock
or following the old adage to "keep the head down"
usually restricts the backswing and shortens your
distance.*

8. Stay Light on Your Feet

When a golfer loses the agility in his legs, he's a cripple. You cannot swing the club at any great speed without the support of your legs. For that reason, you must fight with every fiber of your being to keep your legs strong and healthy. Whenever possible, walk when you play golf; don't ride. Watch your diet and try to stay trim. Exercise your legs whether it be through walking, riding a bicycle or jogging. Keep active.

It is your legs that support the speed of your hands and arms and wrists as they move around your body. If your legs get tired and don't want to move, then the instinctive reaction is to move faster with the upper body to overcome the slowness of the lower body, which makes you throw the club outside the target line, lose the retention of your angle and release the club too early. The player who can still maintain some degree of flexibility and lightness in his lower body to move from one foot to the other, is going to play better golf for a longer period of time. Once you get heavy on your feet, which often can be attributed to gaining weight, it's more difficult to move your legs.

I think it's essential that seniors learn to become toe-and-heel players. By that I mean you should finish your backswing with your left heel off the ground, balanced on the right foot and left toe, and finish your follow-through with the right heel off the ground, balanced on the left foot and right toe. It's a very natural, fluid motion. It's the way you move when you walk—from heel to toe, from heel to toe—yet you probably don't realize it.

Feeling foot pressure on the forward swing

Most golfers don't realize that when the hands and arms move down on the forward swing there is a corresponding action in the lower body. The arms transmit a downward motion to the legs that in turn exert a downward pressure on the feet. The result is a downward foot pressure that accommodates the downward pressure of the hands and arms. Some golfers don't appreciate this law of physics and their feet are going up when their hands are going down. The proper action in the golf swing is similar to the pumping motion in the body of a basketball player dribbling a ball. As the hands and arms move downward the legs and feet accommodate the pumping with a flexing motion. Try to feel this downward pressure exerted on your feet the next time you're hitting practice balls.

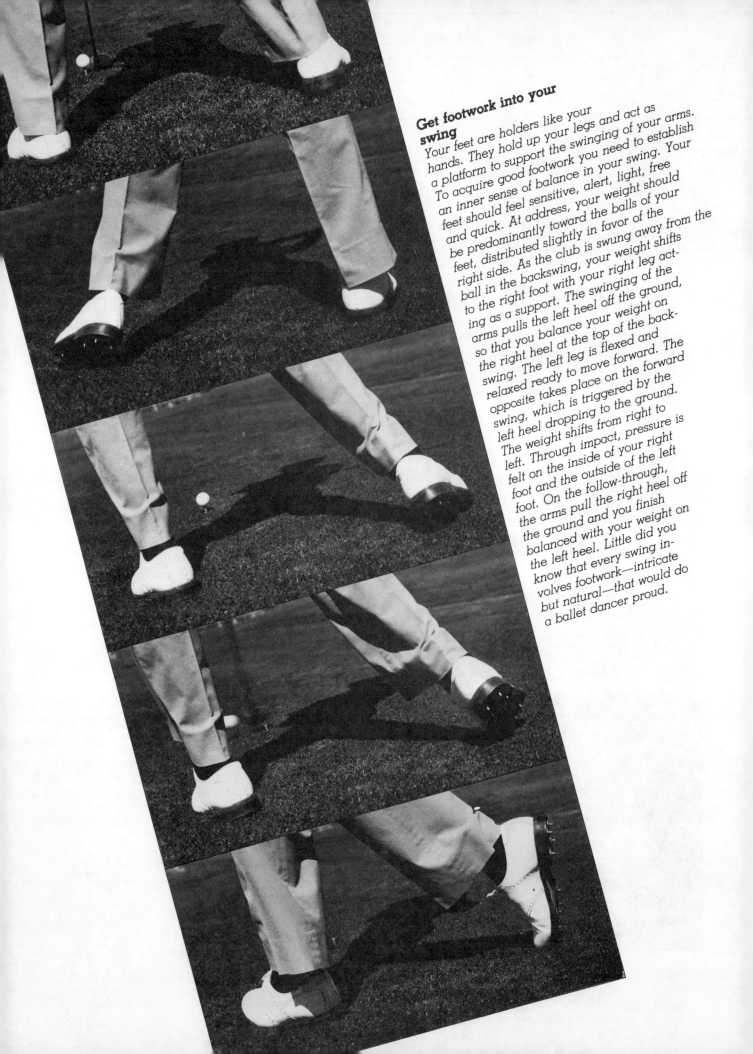

Get footwork into your swing

Your feet are holders like your hands. They hold up your legs and act as a platform to support the swinging of your arms. To acquire good footwork you need to establish an inner sense of balance in your swing. Your feet should feel sensitive, alert, light, free and quick. At address, your weight should be predominantly toward the balls of your feet, distributed slightly in favor of the right side. As the club is swung away from the ball in the backswing, your weight shifts to the right foot with your right leg acting as a support. The swinging of the arms pulls the left heel off the ground, so that you balance your weight on the right heel at the top of the backswing. The left leg is flexed and relaxed ready to move forward. The opposite takes place on the forward swing, which is triggered by the left heel dropping to the ground. The weight shifts from right to left. Through impact, pressure is felt on the inside of your right foot and the outside of the left foot. On the follow-through, the arms pull the right heel off the ground and you finish balanced with your weight on the left heel. Little did you know that every swing involves footwork—intricate but natural—that would do a ballet dancer proud.

Light and lively foot action

Byron Nelson, at age 69, continues to demonstrate wonderfully light foot action throughout the swing. Notice that at impact his right foot is almost completely off the ground, his weight has moved onto the left leg and he remains balanced on the inside of his right instep. The average senior player never transfers his weight off the right foot on the through-swing.

5 2 MIRACLE CURES TO SAVE THE SENIOR SWING

In working with older pupils, I often rely on two simple alterations to help the players achieve quickly in their swings the kind of results I have been advocating and explaining in previous chapters. I call these alterations "miracle cures" because they usually produce immediate and amazing results on the practice tee. By all means try each of them yourself.

1. Move Ball to Center of Your Stance

The first cure is based on the principle that most golfers, especially as they get older, lose some mobility in their lower bodies. They do not play as well from beneath their waist. Let us pause for a moment to consider an experiment. Imagine a golfer at address with three balls on the ground in front of him: the first off his left heel, the second off the middle of his stance and the third off his right heel. Which ball do you think he would hit most consistently if he were not able to transfer his weight? Obviously, the middle ball position. Jack Nicklaus and other tour pros can play the ball forward in their stance because they move their lower bodies and transfer their weight so easily in the swing. If you're finding that you don't drive with your legs and shift your weight as in the old days, try playing the ball back toward the center of your stance. Your first priority should be to catch the ball solidly, and this adjustment will ensure more solid contact.

"You often hear of Jack Nicklaus and other fellows on tour playing all their shots off the left heel, but that takes a tremendous amount of lower body action. One of these days even Nicklaus is going to have to move the ball back in his stance. I recall playing many rounds with Ben Hogan when he was in his late 50s and I can tell you he played every shot from almost center in his stance. That's good enough for me."—Jay Hebert

Peter Kostis, one of my colleagues in the Golf Digest Instruction Schools, believes that you should have to earn the right to play the ball forward in your stance. I'd even go a step further and say that periodically you should have to earn recertification to play the ball forward, sort of like an annual physical examination or car inspection. The test would be pretty simple. On the practice range, using a 5-iron, start with the ball in the middle of your stance and hit a half dozen shots. Then move the ball an inch forward (to the left for

Finding the right ball position
If a golfer does not transfer his weight, which ball position do you think will yield the most consistent results—off his left foot, off the center of his stance or off his right foot? Surely, the center position. If you're having trouble shifting your weight or moving your lower body in the swing, try playing the ball farther back in your stance for more solid contact.

right-handers) and hit another five or six shots observing their dispersion and the quality of contact. Continue moving the ball to the left until you find that you start hitting it fat (contacting the ground before the ball).

I'd still recommend positioning the ball off your left heel with the driver, because it is on a tee and the ideal angle of approach is level to ascending. You want your clubhead moving along the ground or even a couple of degrees upward when it contacts the ball. The worse the lie or the closer the ball is to the ground, the more you want your clubhead traveling downward and forward at impact. The simplest way to achieve a descending blow is to position the ball farther back in your stance at address, which puts your swing center ahead of the ball. Learning to hit your irons on the descent and your driver on the ascent will vastly improve the crispness of your contact and the distance of your shots.

You can learn the feeling of ascent and descent by hitting practice shots from uneven lies. On a downhill lie, feel the clubhead moving downward and forward through the ball, as it should when you make a "descending blow." On an uphill lie, swing the clubhead upward with the contour of the ground and you'll experience an "ascending blow." To round out your education, hit some balls off a level lie. Try to contact the ball with the clubhead moving horizontally along the ground to experience a "level blow."

The rule of thumb: Hit down on the ball when it's down in the grass and hit up on the ball when it's up on a tee.

Swing and sway to add distance and backspin

I'm often asked how to put backspin on the ball. Backspin is a result of the oblique contact of club and ball, meaning that the clubhead is moving downward and forward when it contacts the ball. Backspin, then, is caused by a descending blow. How do you increase descent to get more backspin? By using your lower body more effectively. Your legs should move forward leading the arms and hands down and through the ball. If you told a baseball pitcher to throw a ball without leading with the lower body, he'd lose all his power. The good golfer, as Gene Littler demonstrates here with a 5-iron, generates his power by leading with the lower body. He moves his left knee to the right of the ball on the backswing and his right knee to the right of the ball on the through-swing. The poor player never moves his left knee to the right of the ball on the backswing. He's afraid of swaying. If he moves his lower body he thinks he'll move his upper body. What's the big deal? Go ahead and sway. At least it gets your weight moving in the right direction. You'll find it gives you more solid contact, increases your distance and imparts more backspin to your shots.

2. Raise the Left Heel to Liberate Your Swing

As you swing the club around your body on the backswing, you should feel the shoulders pulling at the hips, the arms pulling at the legs and the hands pulling at the feet. As I've mentioned before, the upper body should feel as if it's connected by elastic bands to the lower body.

In a chain reaction, the left heel is raised from the ground by the swinging of the arms around the body, which in turn lets you swing farther back. This simple act of allowing the left heel to be pulled off the ground on the backswing constitutes what I call my Miracle Cure #2 for the aging golfer. Not only does it increase your swing arc, raising the left heel helps you transfer your weight to the right side on the backswing, giving you maximum leverage to kick off the downswing. Then a reverse chain reaction occurs—the left heel drops to the ground, which drops the hands, which initiates the change of direction.

Keeping the left heel glued to the ground stifles the motion of your lower body in the swing and dramatically cuts down on the length of the backswing, which costs you distance and consistency. On the other hand, you shouldn't lift the left heel in a conscious, independent action; it should be pulled off the ground by the swinging of your hands around your body.

No doubt the greatest proponent of raising the left heel is Jack Nicklaus, who was taught by Jack Grout to "reach for the sky" on the backswing. If you feel that you're reaching for the sky, you'll naturally raise the left heel. Nicklaus has kept his swing tremendously long, which in part accounts for his continued success as he's gone the other side of 40. Nicklaus keeps his lower body free and supple so it can act as the support for the upper body in the swing. When the lower body becomes tense and static, the upper body has to work that much harder. More pressure is exerted on the lower back muscles, the spine, and the wrists and hands.

Seymour Dunn, one of golf's early teachers, once said that the good player swings well from above his waist, but the exceptional player also swings well from below his waist. The legs and feet are what give you longevity in golf. They synchronize the swinging of the arms and hands and ultimately the clubhead.

I like to give every part of my body a chance to do its fair share of the work in the swing, because I'm too small to have it otherwise.

For one reason or another, most senior golfers are in the same predicament; we don't possess the strength and coordination of a Sam Snead. We have to make our whole bodies contribute to the swinging of the club. We don't want one part of the body saying, "Hey, that s.o.b. isn't doing its fair share." If your muscles could think, that's what they'd say. Harmonizing the upper body with the lower body produces longevity.

Art Wall Case Study

Art Wall has always had a relatively flat-footed swing and consequently hits the ball on a low trajectory, not as far as he's capable of. In recent years, he's made a conscious effort to improve the footwork of his swing, with noticeable success.

"I feel like I'm moving better with my lower body. It's a little thing, but it's renewed a lot of my enthusiasm for the game. I've always hung back a little on my right side. I've swung flat-footed and so had to use my hands and arms more than others. Now I seem to be moving my legs better.

"My main thought is to get my left shoulder behind the ball on the backswing and then shift my weight over to my left side on the through-swing. I've never had complete confidence in my game, but now I really do."—Art Wall

The only way Art can get his left shoulder behind, or to the right of, the ball on the backswing is to move freely with his lower body. If the left foot is anchored to the ground, it will resist the swinging of the hands, which in turn cuts off the arm swing, which cuts off the shoulder turn. Art builds up more leverage on his backswing now, because he's allowing his feet and legs to move freely throughout the swing.

Tommy Bolt Case Study

Tommy Bolt is not nearly as competitive as he should be on the senior tour because of a technical flaw in his swing. He has too short a backswing because he doesn't allow his left heel to come off the ground. His left leg is rigid and his left foot is glued down, preventing his arms from swinging farther around his body, increasing his arc and building up clubhead speed. He's losing 20 or 30 yards off his tee shots—the difference between winning and losing in most brackets.

"Toski doesn't know what he's talking about! I've never let my left heel come off the ground, and I don't intend to do it now. I keep it down because it gives me more control. Sure, I've lost distance over the years, but my short game is better than ever. If this senior tour had come along 12 years ago, when I could really play, it would have been super for me.

But a 62-year-old can't compete with a 50-year-old day in and day out. The spring chicken will wear him out."
— Tommy Bolt

Contrary to what Bolt says, he used to lift his left heel on the backswing. Tommy still can play good golf because his body is very strong, and he has tremendous lower body coordination. He's got to have these assets to play from the position he puts himself in at the top of the backswing, well short of parallel. But as he gets older, he'll have more problems. Any inches he adds to his backswing will translate into yards on his tee shots.

6 PICK A SWING MODEL COMPATIBLE WITH YOUR BODY SHAPE & METABOLISM

If a foot race were staged tomorrow between Julius Boros, Gene Littler and Bob Toski, smart money would bet on the little man. In all modesty, I'd have to go off a 9-to-5 favorite. It is a law of nature that light beats might on the running track. The likely order of finish would be Toski (130 pounds), Littler (160 pounds) and Boros (200 pounds).

On the other hand, if a weight-lifting contest were held between the three of us, the big man would have the edge. Boros would win going away and I need not even enter.

Each of us has our own pluses and minuses. The successful player learns to develop a game that emphasizes his strengths and diminishes his weaknesses.

As in most other athletics, there are two forms of power in golf—ponderous strength and quick strength, as my friend Paul Runyan calls them. Let's take boxing as an example. George Foreman, a fighter of ponderous strength if there ever was one, knocked out his opponents with hard, powerful punches. Muhammad Ali, certainly in his younger days a practitioner of quick strength, relied on speed to wear down his opponents. I'm not arguing that one system is better than the other, simply that the good fighter, or the good golfer, finds the system that works for him.

How do you do this? I think you learn best by imitation. Pick a golfer, roughly your own age, who has a comparable body size, and then try to pattern your swing after his. It's also good to choose as a model someone with a metabolism similar to your own. If you're slow-moving and laconic, you don't want to imitate me, for instance. It should be an educational experience picking a swing model and following that person at senior tournaments, on television or, even, through the newspaper. The three models shown in photo sequences in this chapter—while I think ideal for the three basic body sizes—are by no means the only ones you can choose to imitate.

Julius Boros
Height: 6'
Weight: 200 pounds
Born: March 3, 1920

Gene Littler
Height: 5'9½"
Weight: 160 pounds
Born: July 21, 1930

Bob Toski
Height: 5'7"
Weight: 130 pounds
Born: September 18, 1927

1. Julius Boros—a model for the stout golfer

Julius Boros swings a golf club the way the grass grows. The club moves imperceptibly at first, then slowly. There is no great sense of urgency about it. The result is quite certain.

Actually, Boros swings so slowly that it takes about twice as much film to photograph his swing as any of the other pros in this book. The point is that a heavy man naturally moves slower than a light man. Julius weighs 200 pounds and stands six feet tall. If you are similarly proportioned, you would do well to emulate his slow, even tempo.

It's difficult to determine exactly when Boros starts his swing. He has a loose-jointed setup in which he first holds the clubface squarely behind the ball, then he pulls it back so the ball is off the toe, then he slides it forward so the ball is at the heel, then he pushes it sideways away from the ball to begin the backswing. It's the damnedest thing I've ever seen. The whole procedure takes only a few seconds, but the movements occur smoothly, flowingly. Try to do that with a tight grip. You simply can't slide the clubhead around at address as Boros does unless you do it softly and easily, which sets the tone for the whole swing.

Boros is what I consider a "subconscious player." He plays reactively, by feel and touch. If Boros gripped the club tightly or snatched it away quickly, he'd never find the ball.

I don't necessarily advocate his setup mannerisms. However, they force Boros to hold the club lightly and swing it slowly—two characteristics I do advocate.

"Sometimes I grip the club so lightly that I get loose. If I firmed up my grip, I'd probably drive the ball a little farther. My takeaway is a little like Miller Barber's—the hands start first ahead of the club, and then I have to play catch up."—Julius Boros

For every golfer who grips the club too loosely, as Julius says, I must see 100 grip it too tightly. Boros is correct, though, in his assessment of his takeaway. As he pushes the clubhead away from the ball, he appears to tilt slightly to the left, staying over the ball longer and not shifting to the right as much as other good players. He starts the clubface back closed to the swing path, and then, after his arms reach about waist height, he rotates the clubface open. His backswing in these respects is indeed similar to Miller Barber's; both of them take unorthodox routes to reach the top, but once there they are copybook perfect.

Boros, for a heavy man, is amazingly supple. He starts with his weight evenly distributed at address and moves onto his right leg, braced to support his upper torso on the backswing. Although he lifts his heel only slightly on the backswing, he is still flexible enough to make a full turn, almost reaching parallel at the top.

For most heavy-set seniors who don't have Boros' strength and suppleness, I'd recommend setting more weight on the right side at address, which gives you a head start to shift to the right on the backswing and assume a position of leverage to move to the left on the through-swing. You might even try to feel that you're rotating your trunk, or shifting your stomach, to the right on the back-swing—supported by the right leg—and to the left on the through-swing—supported by the left leg. This is a good thought for the overweight golfer.

"My suggestion to a golfer my size is: Lose 40 pounds! When that's not practicable, face up to the fact that the more weight you carry, the harder it is to turn. You can't possibly get the full extension of a skinny player like Don January, but you have to try. Just keep extending farther and farther. And, there is an advantage to size if along with it you have strength. Many big golfers have strong wrists and hands. If that's the case, use more hand and wrist action in your swing."—Julius Boros

Julius Boros' swing philosophy is perhaps best summed up in the title of an instruction book he once wrote—"*Swing Easy, Hit Hard.*" By that, he means you should swing the club at a leisurely pace and then snap your wrists at the right time, presumably through impact.

JULIUS BOROS – A MODEL FOR THE STOUT GOLFER

He just lets his arms swing slowly and freely on the downswing and when they get to the bottom the wrists snap quickly through the ball. He sets the club in motion and lets it go. Al Geiberger, another accomplished tour player, expressed the same thought in a different way: "You only have one fast moment in your swing," he said. "Don't waste it."

Boros is a wonderful hand-and-wrist player. He doesn't so much hit the ball with his arms and his body as other more elegant players. He relies on the timing of the speed muscles of his hands and wrists, complemented by the support muscles of his arms, shoulders and legs. He generates tremendous clubhead speed through the ball. Take note of the quick crossover of his right forearm over the left after impact—that's what I call wrist snap. A lot of teachers today deny there's wrist snap in the swing, which is like denying there's foot action or leg action or hip action or arm action or shoulder action. Every one of these parts of the body plays a role in the swing. The key is to use them in the proper sequence, which is called timing. Boros has such good timing because he has good tempo. Tempo, or pace, creates timing, not the other way around. Without tempo, you can't have good timing.

2. Gene Littler—a model for the average size golfer

Like the vintage cars he tinkers with in his spare time, Gene Littler has grown better with age. He possesses, in my opinion, the finest swing in senior golf. I've watched him play for 25 years now and Gene has always had a very simple swing. He takes the club away and returns it on the same path every time, giving you the impression on the practice tee that each shot is a carbon copy of the one before—surely the reason for his nickname, "The Machine." I think he's a more consistent swinger of the club today because he has better control of his left wrist, hand and arm throughout the swing. He's in a very solid position at the top of the backswing, which wasn't always true. He used to have a little hitch at the top, but now he's smooth as silk changing directions.

At 5-foot-9½ and 160 pounds, Gene is the perfect model for the average-size senior golfer. But not only is his effortless swing worth copying, Littler's inner spirit teaches all of us the greater lesson. In the spring of 1972, he underwent surgery for cancer of the lymph glands, and it appeared that his career as a tournament player might be over. But Littler came back to win five more tournaments on the PGA Tour and today dominates play on the senior tour. A man who conquered cancer finds advancing age no match for his indomitable spirit.

"One of the reasons I wasn't sure I wanted to play senior golf was I feared the emphasis would be on how old everybody is. I'm not saying I play like I'm a kid, but I don't want to think old. Everybody seems to believe that when you're 50 or 60 you automatically can't turn and do the things you did when you were younger. I think that's hogwash. If you do some simple stretching exercises and keep your body supple, there's no reason you can't make a full turn and hit it nearly as well as when you were younger."—Gene Littler

Aside from his desire to remain competitive, Littler's longevity stems from the lyrical tempo of his swing. His philosophy is that you swing every club in your bag at the same pace, from the driver to the wedge. If tempo is the heartbeat of the golf swing, Littler's pulse rate is slow and steady.

GENE LITTLER – A MODEL FOR THE AVERAGE SIZE GOLFER

"I try to concentrate on smoothness and rhythm as I prepare to hit the ball. I take a couple of practice swings and then attempt to repeat that same relaxed tempo. The first foot or so of the takeaway sets the pace—you have to be smooth there."—Gene Littler

Littler doesn't precock his head at address, but rather turns it to the right as he swings the club away from the ball. Notice in the accompanying photographs that his head slides to the right, over his right knee, on the backswing. The head should move freely in the swing as long as it stays to the right of the ball. (I don't like to say "behind the ball," because only the clubhead at address is truly behind the ball). With the head turned to the right, you are in what I term the power position.

Littler looks very strong at the top of his backswing. The slow pace at which he swings back keeps his hands and arms in control of the club at the top, holding the shaft parallel with the target line. Like most successful senior players, Gene makes a full backswing.

"My swing is longer than it was when I started playing golf. I didn't particularly try to lengthen it, but I'm glad it is. A longer swing lasts longer."— Gene Littler

Where do you think Littler's weight is concentrated at the top of his backswing? Many golfers try to keep their weight on the inside of the right foot, but, as you may observe in these photographs, Gene seems to allow his weight to move slightly to the outside. This is one of the keys for more distance. Don't be afraid to sway on the backswing. Golfers who are too intent on keeping their weight on the inside of the right foot have a tendency to "lean left" and make a reverse weight shift.

"Good footwork promotes good tempo. When my tempo is good, I almost feel I'm swinging the club with my feet. I've always liked the way Sam Snead seems to start his downswing with his feet. The top part of his body doesn't appear to move until after his feet start."—Gene Littler

If you want to see a clear, concise illustration of how the legs support the swing, how they influence the way the ball is struck, look at this man's slacks on the downswing. Starting when the arms reach waist level, you see a violent swishing of creases in Littler's pants legs, which is caused by the rotary action of the hips and thighs turning through impact. Then just as suddenly the slacks are quiet again on the follow-through. It's a graphic demonstration of the velocity generated by the lower body.

The force of his hands, wrists and arms swinging through the ball naturally turn the hips out of the way. "Clearing the hips," as it's called, is really a reaction to the speed muscles of the hands, wrists and arms. He is not trying to turn his chest to the target, as many golfers try to do. Facing the hole on the finish is a reaction to an action. When people try to turn their bodies to the hole, they tend to lose arm speed. Don't worry about where your chest is pointing. Just swing through with vigor, as Gene so ably demonstrates.

3. Bob Toski—a model for the diminutive golfer

I chose myself as the model for seniors of small stature because, at 5-foot-7 and 130 pounds (soaking wet), I am the shortest/lightest player active on the senior tour. I use the quickness of my body to offset any deficiency I may have in strength, which is what players of slight build should do.

I set up with what I call a "wide bipod"—in other words, a wider stance than normal. This gives me a stronger base from which to swing the club and gain leverage. The small, thin golfer who is very flexible doesn't need a narrow stance to make a full turn; what he needs is a wide stance to give him better balance. His physique naturally allows him to make a longer, faster swing. If he doesn't use a wider bipod at address he runs the risk of falling off balance or tilting to the left as the arms swing up and around his body.

I think it's essential that the small golfer appear alive and alert at address. He has to look like he's ready to hit the ball, not like he's going to tap it. I try to feel like I'm about to take it back and knock the daylights out of the ball.

Take note of the address position: head is cocked to the right; stance is slightly closed; the body is bent from the waist and flexed at the knees; arms are extended but relaxed, with the right arm slightly lower than the left; right knee is kicked in a bit, indicating weight is 60 percent on the right side; hands are forward of the center of the body but inside the left knee, and the ball is positioned off the left heel.

I swing the club away from the ball in a low, wide arc. No attempt is made to take the club back quickly or pick it off the ground abruptly. I use the takeaway to build momentum slowly. I transfer more weight to the right on the backswing, winding around the right leg to build torque with the upper body. It's relatively easy for me to turn because my body is so small and light.

If I swing the club back too fast, the coiling of my upper body pulls my right leg to the left and I tilt back to the target. My wrists and arms are not strong enough to sustain the speed of my arms and hands winding up, which is why the club goes past horizontal at the top of my backswing and crosses the target line. However, this isn't all bad. It's a position I can create a lot of power from if the legs move first to initiate the downswing.

The downswing is triggered by the left heel, which was raised on the backswing, now dropping to the ground to begin the flow of weight from right to left. The first move by the upper body is the turning of the shoulders. Because the shoulders are among the heaviest muscles used in the swing, they need a head start on the downswing. Then the race to the ball follows in sequence with the arms, wrists and hands. The big muscles complement the little muscles. The senior golfer must learn to time the speed muscles of the hands and wrists with the support muscles of the shoulders, arms and legs to generate maximum force in the swing.

Another good thought for the senior is to feel the right arm working under the left arm, both on the backswing and the downswing. The right arm doesn't work over the left until after the ball is hit. Many golfers cross the right over the left well before impact.

Wrist action is a vital source of power for the diminutive golfer, but only if it's used in the proper sequence. The arms cannot stop while the wrists snap through impact. The arms must keep moving, leading the hands in the race to the ball. If the arms decelerate and are overtaken by the hands, you'll tend to throw the clubhead outside the target line and cut across the ball, greatly diminishing your power. It is the cause also of seniors finishing their swing at waist high with the arms close to their body. If the arms continue to move as you shift your weight from right to left, you'll naturally swing them away from your body.

The feeling I have when I go through the ball on a good shot is that my hands are trying to swing away from my shoulders. I feel as if my arms are made of rubber and they're stretching away. Then on the follow-through, they snap back again. Retention on the downswing creates extension on the forward swing and that generates clubhead speed and powerful shots.

The left wrist is probably the weaker of your two wrists so it must be supported by the left arm in the swing. I've always said that you can't fire your right side until you have the left side under control. It's like the fighter who must learn to use his left before he can hit with the right; he must jab with his left first and then punch with the right.

A good exercise to develop wrist strength and speed is to grip the club with the left hand and then put your right hand over the left, with no part of the right touching the grip. Start hitting shots with the ball teed high on a peg and then gradually lower it. Practice this

BOB TOSKI–A MODEL FOR THE DIMINUTIVE GOLFER

drill trying to draw the ball and making a descending blow.

The story of my leg action is told by the creases in the pants legs. I make an aggressive rotary action through the ball with legs and hips led by the swinging of my arms and hands. Observe also that my head is still to the right of the ball at impact, which helps deliver a fast blow from the inside squarely down the target line. The photos show how quickly I get off the right foot on the forward swing. Most golfers don't get over to the left foot and hang back on the right much too long in the swing, which retards clubhead speed. Think of getting off the right foot and onto the left quickly on the downswing and you'll increase clubhead speed and distance.

7 SHARPEN YOUR SHORT GAME —BY MAKING IT LONGER!

The trouble with the average senior player's short game is that it is too short. Don't be afraid to knock the ball to the hole. It seems to me that everybody comes up short. This is true in full approaches as well as partial shots around the green. Many seniors play scared golf. They sneak up on the ball. They stop their swings midway through impact. Steering the ball is a problem with every aspect of the game, but none more so than the shots near the hole—chips, pitches and bunker play. You must learn to play boldly and swing the club briskly through the ball. Don't tighten your wrists and hands on the downswing and retard clubhead speed at impact. Let your hands and arms swing through the ball.

In this chapter, I've selected senior pros who excel in the short game to demonstrate their techniques so that you can study the pictures and try to duplicate their finer points.

One general thought first. My motto has always been "minimum air time and maximum ground time." I recommend rolling the ball on the ground as soon as possible. Don't try to cut a wedge in close to the flag when a run-up 7-iron will do the job more consistently. Take the least lofted club that will get the ball rolling on level ground and hit it hard enough to send the ball to the hole. Don't be short.

1. Chipping—Bob Rosburg

Bob Rosburg, long considered an up-and-down artist, advocates a sharp descending blow on chip shots. He plays the ball well back in his stance and sets most of his weight on the left leg. To strike the ball with descent, the grip end of the club must precede the clubhead through impact, so Bob also presets his hands ahead of the ball at address. "The worse the lie of the ball, the more I favor my left side to steepen the angle," he says.

Rosburg makes an abbreviated backswing and then "pops" down on the ball, leading with a firm left arm. It's actually a tap or punch stroke. I like the way he cocks his wrists on the backswing, putting the clubhead in position to strike down and through the ball, but I don't like the way he's hooded or closed the clubface. The chip should be a mini-swing, with the clubface opening on the backswing, squaring up at impact and then closing on the follow-through.

Rosburg makes a sharp swing down and through the ball and finishes with the left wrist firm and intact. Many seniors tend to scoop the ball and finish with a collapsed left wrist. Try to emulate Rosburg's brisk motion through the ball and you'll make crisper contact with more consistent results.

3

4

2. Pitching—Art Wall

Art Wall sets up for the pitch shot with about 55 percent of his weight on the left side and the ball positioned in the center of his stance. The key to his graceful pitching motion is the dominance of his left arm, which stays relatively straight but relaxed throughout the stroke. He sets the angle early on the backswing, cocking his wrists quickly to raise the clubhead into the air. The lesson here is that you cannot hit down until you first get the clubhead up. From the top of the backswing, he leads with his left arm to strike down and through the ball. The left arm stabilizes the blow of the left hand and wrist against the ball and the right arm doesn't cross over until well after impact. Art has a wonderful touch with this shot and is probably the best pitcher on the senior tour. "I practice my short game a lot," he says. "I know I have a good short game as long as I practice it. I'm always thinking about it a little. It's always in the back of my mind."

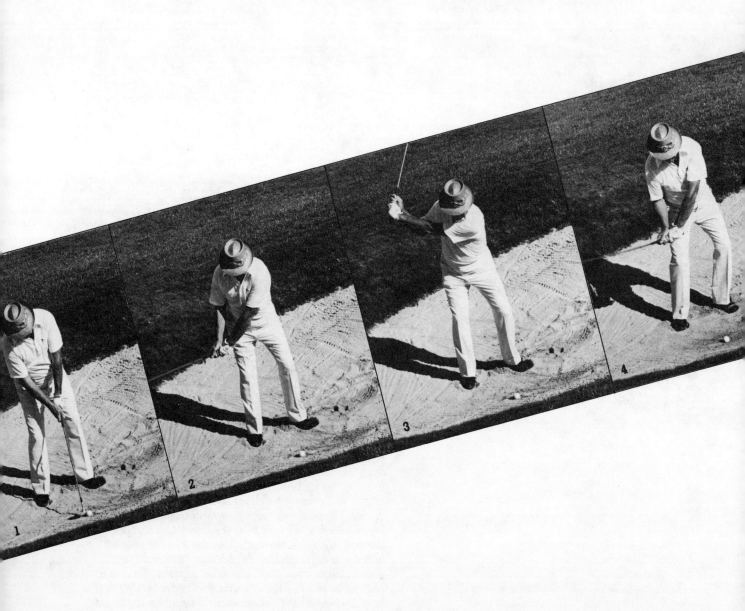

3. Long Bunker Shot—Sam Snead

What the average golfer has never understood about a bunker shot is that the arms swing to the side of the body more than around the body. The swing is very upright. The clubhead travels almost vertically on the backswing, then moves downward into the sand and underneath the ball, then moves upward in the same manner on the follow-through. The average golfer tries to swing the club around his body in a rotary action and drives it downward into the ball cutting deeply into the sand, with inconsistent results.

Observe how Sam Snead, in these photographs, swings his arms to the side of his body. It's important to note on the long bunker shot that Sam's arm position at the top of the backswing reaches the same height as the finish of his through-swing.

"The arc is the whole thing in playing from the sand trap," he says. "You've got to get the arc going up and down on the same line. If you lay it off or come over the top or duck down, your shot is usually screwed up. But if you swing on the same path up and down, you're usually in good shape."

Snead looks so at ease playing this bunker shot, in stark contrast to the appearance of most seniors in the sand. The reason, of course, is that Snead has a clear conception of the arc he's trying to create while the average player is just guessing. Sam as always swings with such grace, allowing the weight of the club to do the work. The senior usually fights his arms and hands and disrupts the momentum of the club.

Notice also that Sam even cocks his head to the right in playing from the sand. Good habits are hard to break. Because this is a fairly long bunker shot (approximately 60 feet), he shows a pronounced flex in his knees through impact. Many players tend to straighten up on the downswing and scoop the ball. Sam moves his lower body well on the downswing and keeps the right arm working under the left. The right wrist and hand cross over the left only after impact.

4. Short Bunker Shot—Gardner Dickinson

Gardner Dickinson plays this short bunker shot (approximately 30 feet) with an open stance and an open clubface. The senior golfer should realize that, unless the ball is buried, all sand shots are played with an open blade to allow the "bounce" of the club to work. A good sand wedge has a wide sole with a trailing edge that's lower than the leading edge of the clubface. This configuration gives the club a rudder-like action through the sand, preventing it from cutting in deeply.

Notice that Dickinson sets his wrists early in the swing as he moves the clubhead upward. Gardner swings his arms on almost a vertical path. At the top of the backswing, his hands are in front of his chest, rather than behind his body.

On the downswing, he doesn't use a lot of leg and foot action, because it's a very short shot and he doesn't have to generate much clubhead speed. Observe how his head remains under control through the swing, but then he allows it to rise up after impact. His arms are soft and relaxed, free of tension. There's no effort to scoop or force the shot. He's letting the weight of the clubhead fall and accelerate through the sand. On the follow-through, his arms again move upward in a vertical action and his hands finish in front of his chest.

8 RE-LEARN TO PUTT LIKE A KID

Do you remember the days when you didn't think you could miss a putt? When we were young and just taking up golf, most of us found putting pretty easy, even fun. But as we've grown older and discovered putts could be missed, it's probably become the hardest segment of the game for us to master. After much study of the subject, I'm convinced that the problems most seniors have with putting are strictly mental. I've had the opportunity to watch many great putters over the years and one thing I've noticed is a similiarity in attitude. No matter how difficult the putt, every great player gave me the impression he knew he was going to make it. Poor players always appear less certain and more concerned with how they're going to miss it.

"I have a lot of confidence in my putting ability. When I get over the ball, I'm not trying to think of a way to miss it. I'm figuring I can't miss it. If I do miss, it surprises the hell out of me. If you think you're going to make everything, you are going to make more putts.

"Too many players worry about their grip or their stroke. I never think mechanics on the green. I think about what's between me and the hole and what the putt's going to do. I block out everything else." —Harvie Ward

Dan Sikes proposes a theory that the yips are always a mental problem, actually caused by laziness. The yips, of course, are that dreaded affliction of the nervous system that turns grown men into shivering bowls of jelly when faced with short putts.

"Most yippers don't want to accept the challenge of making another three- or four-foot putt. It takes a lot of mental effort to make a putt, and they're not willing to work at it. Play golf for 30 years and suddenly you get tired of the pressure of putting. The easy

way out is to say, 'I have the yips and I don't want to handle this pressure any more.' "—Dan Sikes

It has been widely reported in the press that the yips are a golfer's form of hardening of the arteries, that they torment only the senior player. Actually, every golfer, no matter what his age, is susceptible to the hated yips. I once made the mistake of asking Sam Snead why he thought he missed so many three-foot putts. "Mouse," he said, as if I should have known better, "I've hit the ball three feet from the hole more than anybody, so naturally I'm gonna miss more." Now that's a positive attitude.

Don't allow a bad putting day to shake your confidence. Confidence is nothing more or less than a success pattern. You can only create a success pattern with the putter by thinking positively and believing you can do it.

I think there are three reasons for the yips: (1) the silence of the game, (2) the lack of motion in putting, and (3) the small size of the hole. In every other sport, you are in motion during play and usually there's noise in the background. You won't ever see a basketball player or tennis player yip a shot. But in golf you're standing totally static over the ball and there's so much silence around you that your awareness factor enters in. You begin to wonder who's watching, what they're thinking, and if you're going to embarrass yourself. The added element that the hole is so small serves to heighten all these fears. The way to combat the yips is to follow Harvie Ward's advice: "Block out everything except what's between you and the hole, and believe you can make it."

Some seniors have told me that their putting woes are a result of a weakening of their legs over the ball.

"At times I feel a little unsteady on my feet. When I was younger, I never felt any motion addressing a putt. I also didn't have to look through eyeglasses. This lack of steadiness is the one thing that bothers me in putting. I feel as though I'm moving and wavering over the ball. I may not be, but that's the feeling I have. I don't feel balanced."—Byron Nelson

I have never found steadiness on my feet to be a problem, so this is difficult for me to relate to. My putting problems are usually on the first few holes when I'm still nervous, but my legs are fresh. Of course, I don't have much weight to carry, either. I know that when I do feel an unsteadiness—in the wind, for example—widening the bipod, or the stance, gives me a more secure base.

The up-and-coming way to putt is sidesaddle a la Sam Snead. There's no doubt in my mind it's more technically sound than the conventional putting method. Facing the hole has two undeniable advantages: First, it makes lining up more accurate, because as in other target sports you're standing behind the projectile instead of to its side. And second, it virtually eliminates any twisting of the clubface off line, because the putter swings like a pendulum—straight back and through—not opening and closing as in the conventional system.

"Putting sidesaddle takes the twitch out of your stroke. It uses the big muscles of the right arm and shoulder to swing the putter, which act as an extension of the shaft itself. In the normal stroke, the putter is moved more by the fingers and wrists—and they're the critters that are prone to get nervous. With the sidesaddle stroke, you keep the right arm straight—not bent at the elbow—and just swing it back and forth. You'll find it easier to accelerate through the ball and hit the sweet spot more consistently."—Sam Snead

After much experimentation, I've recently switched to the sidesaddle method and now can tell you from first-hand experience that it works. I pretty much use the same technique as Snead. I hold the butt end of the putter in my left hand with my thumb over the top, pointing toward the hole. I hold the club in the middle of the shaft with my right hand, with the palm facing in the same direction as the putterface. I bend from the hips and stand with my right foot slightly in front of my left, to the side of the target line. The left hand acts as a fulcrum to stabilize the swinging of the putterhead by the right arm. The action is similar to throwing a ball underhanded—the right palm swings back and through, facing the target at all times, thus keeping the putterface on line.

You'll have to experiment yourself with the sidesaddle method to arrive at the precise technique that works for you, but I guarantee it will be time well spent. Your club pro can rig up your current putter for sidesaddle by extending the grip down the shaft or adding a second grip in the middle of the shaft. I recommend it highly. The difficult part is becoming accustomed to seeing the hole from behind the ball. It'll take a while to acclimate your stroke and gain confidence in the method, so don't quit until you've given it a fair test.

Putting sidesaddle

Sam Snead, the father of sidesaddle putting, holds the butt end of the club in his left hand and the middle of the shaft in the palm of his right hand. He bends at the hips, flexes at the knees and stands with his right foot in front of the left, to the side of the target line. The stroke is a simple exercise in engineering. The left hand remains stationary like a fulcrum and the right arm swings the putter like a pendulum.

Another sidesaddle technique

George Bayer uses a hybrid form of sidesaddle putting. He grips the putter with his left hand similar to Snead, but holds the shaft in the fingers of his right hand like a pencil. "I'll never switch back to conventional," says Bayer. "I should have gone to sidesaddle 25 years ago. It's brought my putts per round down from 35 to about 30. It's a whole new life for me. I like it better than conventional because it stops me from turning my upper body on the stroke, which twists the blade open or closed. That doesn't happen any more because my arm just swings back and through on the target line."

An open stance lets you see the hole better
Art Wall, one of the senior tour's preeminent putters, sets up to the ball with an open stance, which gives him a better view of the hole. His eyeline is directly over the ball, another principle of good putting. He has a better view of the line of the putt and he's able to swing his arms close to his body. The farther you stand from the ball, the more you have to rotate the club around your body, thus encountering a higher probability of error.

1   2   3

1   2

4

5

4

5

Putting like 'The Machine'

If you prefer to use the conventional putting method, you can find no better model than Gene Littler, who is one of the best putters in senior golf.

"I try to take the hands out of the stroke," says Gene. "I like to set up square with the target line and swing more with my arms and shoulders. It seems to me that you control your big muscles a lot better than you do the small muscles. The hands and wrists will desert you coming down the stretch under pressure."

I have to disagree with Gene when he talks about taking the hands out of the stroke. Gene does swing the putter mostly with his arms, but the club is connected to his hands and they play a part too. Observe the length of Littler's long, fluid backswing. No short, quick stroke here. He forces nothing. He makes a beautiful, full stroke and lets the pendulum motion of the clubhead roll the ball.

Notice that his wrists break down after impact, his right hand passing the left. The poor golfer allows his wrists to break down before impact. But Littler doesn't try to force his wrists to stay too firm, which could cause him to push the ball. He allows them to unhinge, but at the right moment, which is what I consider good hand action.

9 SHREWD SENIOR STRATEGIES: HOW TO PRACTICE, PREPARE ...AND PREVAIL

Sportswriter: Roberto, you seem to be doing a lot of practicing today.
DeVicenzo: I need it.
Sportswriter: How many practice balls do you normally hit?
DeVicenzo: 500 to 800.
Sportswriter: How often do you do that?
DeVicenzo: Every day.
Sportswriter: How long have you been doing that?
DeVicenzo: Forever.

This exchange with Roberto de Vicenzo, Argentina's rejoinder to Sam Snead, illustrates quite starkly the secret to longevity: Never give it up and practice like hell. Now I don't believe that Roberto hits 500-800 balls every day, but it's a nice story. He probably hits a couple of hundred, which is still a lot. And his mind is never far from the game.

There's nothing like practice to keep your game fine-tuned. But practice shouldn't be construed to mean hard work. Practice involves time—a consistent effort to put forth time and apply yourself mentally to the process of improvement. Hard work has nothing to do with it. Work, to me, is when you take a shovel and dig a ditch or swing a sledgehammer. Pitching, chipping and putting are not work. A little bit of practice on the short game goes a long way. It's the area where improvement is reflected on your scorecard the quickest.

"I never used to practice the short game when I was younger. I'd rather hit 2-irons on the range, but looking back on it the 2-iron was not a very useful club. Nowadays I try to spend more time practicing chips, bunker shots, pitches, putts. That area is where your inadequacies really show up on the golf course."—Jay Hebert

But the majority of golfers would rather talk about their games at the 19th hole than go out to the practice tee and do something about them. Practice can and should be fun, if you do it properly. Nothing says you can't practice on the golf course with a couple of balls, but play by yourself so you can concentrate on what you're working on. Don't go out and try to hustle somebody in a $5 nassau and call it practice.

I try to make my practice sessions more fun by experimenting with different types of shots. Good players are innovators on the course. They know how to improvise an unusual shot to fit each situation. But they just don't go out on the course and try shots off the top of their head in competition. They've done their homework and hit a mountain of balls in practice in order to have the vision and coordination to pull off a particular shot when it counts. Apportion time in your next practice session to try different types of pitches and chips and knock-down shots, from different types of lies. Learn to bend your shots left-to-right and right-to-left.

"I've found that I have to work harder as I've gotten older. I have to practice more. It's just the opposite of what most people would think—that after you've played golf for 30 years and logged as many hours on the practice tee as I have, hitting millions of balls, that you should have it perfected by now. But it takes me longer to get the tempo and feel now than it did 25 years ago."—Gene Littler

This talk of practice reminds me of the time I was standing on the practice range with Lloyd Mangrum at the St. Paul Open. In those days, the caddies used to shag the balls and every pro had his own shag bag. Mangrum was not much of a practicer and he had a very small shag bag indeed. This guy in the gallery yelled out to Lloyd, "How come you don't hit as many practice balls as that little guy over there (meaning me)." Mangrum said, "He's still looking for it and I've already found it." Then this guy said, "You used to be a great player, didn't you?" And Mangrum said, "Better to have been a has-been than a never-was. What's your claim to fame?" By this time the guy was embarrassed and he said, "I work in a bakery." Lloyd sidled over to me with a sly grin and said, "I guess I straightened that cat out." Lloyd was a horrible senior golfer.

Prepare your mind and body to play the game

Preparation for a round of golf should start the night before. I need eight to ten hours of sleep. This obviously varies with the individual, but the body does need time to regenerate itself. I think most seniors find themselves going to bed earlier now than when they were younger. This is another aspect of my basic senior philosophy that we should slow down the tempo of our lives as we grow older. Not only should we take longer to swing the club, we need more time to sleep the night before we swing that club.

The mornings of the days I play golf, I like to get up at least a couple of hours before my starting time. Then I make a special effort to slow down the pace of my morning rites—brushing my teeth, shaving, showering, exercising, eating breakfast, etc. By the time I'm ready to go to the course, my body is on cruise control.

If at all possible, avoid driving to the course yourself. I'd rather have someone else do the driving so I don't have to worry about traffic. I like to plan to get to the course at least an hour before teeing off. When Julius Boros drives to the course himself, he likes to park as far from the clubhouse as possible, so he can unravel his nerves with a leisurely walk to the locker room. Likewise, Sam Snead prefers to drive very slowly to the course ("So don't get behind me if you're in a hurry," he says).

Once at the club, my only advice is that you maintain this slow pace. You have to learn your own strengths and weaknesses so you don't hit too many practice balls and tire out your body. I know my limit is 30 minutes on the practice range, then I'm ready to go. I would stress that you should hit some practice shots to loosen up the joints. Again, allow more time than you used to, and never rush the warm-up.

Then I like to go over to the putting green and hit a dozen or so practice putts to get a feel for the speed of the greens. Some golfers like to time their practice so they immediately walk from the putting clock to the first tee. Paul Runyan, for one, likes to be hitting drives on the practice tee when they call out his name. My preference is to take 10 or 15 minutes to relax and settle down.

If you need relaxation time before a round, make sure you stay away from tension. Associate only with people who make you feel comfortable. Don't get involved in situations that are bound to make you uptight or nervous. Don't argue with your wife, for instance.

Sam Snead says that for this reason he would never play gin rummy prior to a round of golf. "It got me all tensed up inside," he says. Finally, make sure all of your equipment is in order, your caddie is ready, and whatever other chores you must perform are taken care of. Eliminate any possible sources of irritation.

Prior to a round I sometimes take a hot shower and then a cold one to loosen up my muscles and wake me up. If you try this, give your body plenty of time to recuperate—at least half an hour before you play. Sometimes when my back is giving me trouble, I take a massage before a round. At the Legends of Golf, they have a trainer in the locker room who's worked on some of us seniors with great success. I remember the first year I talked Doc Middlecoff into having a massage and he played some of his best golf in a long time.

As far as drinking or eating before a round is concerned, just use common sense. Stick with light foods; soup and salads are best. You know whether or not an alcoholic drink will adversely affect your play. Middlecoff used to have a pop before a round, and Boros might have a beer. Bobby Jones was a great sipper of scotch. That's just their way of relaxing. They did it in moderation.

Outsmarting the youngsters

I believe I came of age as a golfer along about the back nine of the final round of the World Championship in 1954. We were playing for $50,000, and I had a six-stroke lead over Jackie Burke through the first five holes. Then my game started to come apart at the seams. In the next nine holes there was a nine-stroke swing and Burke led me by three. I had choked like a dog and it was a miserable feeling.

Then suddenly, out of the blue, it occurred to me that so much money can make anybody choke any time. I figured that I just choked early. Maybe the rest of them would choke late.

As it turned out, I went eagle-par-par-birdie on the last four holes and Jackie finished bogey-par-par-par, and I won the tournament and the $50,000 by a single stroke.

I had matured pretty quickly that afternoon in Chicago, fighting for my competitive life at Tam O'Shanter. It taught me the lesson that the breaks go both ways, and if you wait patiently they'll come your way, too.

"You just have to wait your turn. Bobby Locke told me after one practice round, 'Master, you've got to learn how to relax. Try counting to three. One, two, three. You've got to have patience.' Well, that's always been one of my faults. I've never had much patience with myself. We'd all like to be as good as Nicklaus, Snead or Littler, but I realize now that's impossible. If we were that good, they'd find a way to be better."—Bob Goalby

People always talk about the disadvantages of growing older. I'd like to mention the one over-riding advantage of age. I'm just plain smarter now than I ever was—and don't you think that hasn't helped my golf game. I have a more realistic understanding of my strengths and weaknesses. I know my swing, and, when it goes off track, I know why. I understand how to play more types of shots. I know when to gamble and when to play safe. But most of all I know myself, which wasn't always the case.

As I've mentioned before, I am an emotional person and I don't think there's anything wrong with that. However, you have to be able to control your emotions, which I think comes more easily with age. It's all right to get a little hot and let off steam when you make a bad shot—but keep your mind and body under control. Don't allow yourself to get so emotionally high or low that your swing gets too fast or your putting stroke becomes jerky or you can't concentrate on the next shot. When your emotions get out of control to the point where you lose that fine sense of rhythm and touch, then you know your body chemistry has gotten the best of you.

Some people never learn to control their emotions. The senior golfer should have an edge over his younger opponents, because he's had more time to know himself. We should learn from the years of experience that we've had on and off the course, from the exposure we've had to better players. But some of us never really learn—much to our own detriment. For instance, Tommy Bolt, in my opinion, has never changed. I don't think he's compiled the record he deserved. Because of his emotional intensity, his dramatic flair for showmanship on the course, he has had a rather unsuccessful career compared with what might have been. His legendary temper detracted from his ability to play the game—and, oh my, could he play the game. His record is actually poor considering his ability as a player. I say this not to run down Tommy or his golf game but rather as a compliment, because he should have won five National Opens instead of one and he should have won five Masters instead of none. His potential was that great. But I don't think his composure and self-awareness and concentrated effort nearly equalled his physical ability to swing the club.

The senior player should be able to keep his game in perspective, going about his round calmly and quietly, with ease and grace and rhythm. I am reminded of Dr. Cary Middlecoff's approach to the pressure of a three-foot putt. "I know that regardless of whether or not I make it," he said, "my wife still loves me, I have a nice home and I'll still eat steak for dinner." This was Doc's way of keeping the game in perspective. He thought that way winning two U.S. Opens.

Yet sometimes we put so much pressure on ourselves in golf that it drains us mentally and fatigue sets in. Seniors are not that much more susceptible to fatigue in a round of golf than younger players, but it is a pitfall they should be aware of. Fatigue in golf can be caused by anxiety, uncertainty, lack of confidence, self-doubt, and worrying. The player who doesn't worry, or who plays with confidence and a sense of ease about himself, is the player who is not going to wear down during a round. The player who tends to be very intense, anxious and temperamental is prone to run out of gas on the back nine.

"The key is to stay in control of the ball, not let it get away from you. I've found that golf, in this sense, is like tennis—the game doesn't start until the serve gets in. Golf only starts after the tee shot. You have to hit the ball in the fairway. It is not a game of how far, but how near. It's not driving away, but approaching close."—Peter Thomson

Julius Boros in my opinion is the best "control" golfer who ever lived. I've never seen him once reach beyond his grasp on the golf course. He plays entirely within himself. He just puts his ball in the fairway, goes and finds it, and knocks it on the green. At least, that's the impression he gives.

On tour we used to call him "The Moose," because he just kept plodding along on an even keel, never getting excited, never getting mad about a missed shot. He was no doubt one of the best U.S. Open players of all time because of this level temperament. In one 13-year stretch, Boros made the top five in the Open eight times, including winning it twice (1952 and 1963).

"You have to have the right mental approach to the game. Just go out and play. If you have a bad hole—I know it's pretty hard to forget it—but just try to push it aside. It's a matter of keeping the same rhythm through the whole round. If you're playing well and you have a bad hole, don't think you've

Bob Toski and golf's two most celebrated seniors, Arnold Palmer and Sam Snead.

blown the round—just go on to the next hole and use the same old swing and make three or four pars in a row. Never panic. Just keep playing."—Julius Boros

In closing this book, if I may indulge in a bit of sentiment, I would like to recount the first time I played with golf's two most celebrated seniors.

The first time I played with Arnold Palmer was in the 1954 Azalea Open. He was an amateur at the time, and this was his first experience with "big-time" pro golf. In the first round, I was paired with Palmer and Ted Kroll. He later told me that Ted and I left him with a good impression of the pro league. But the point is that Arnie shot 65 in the first round, and he left us with a good impression, too. I can still remember Ted saying, "Let's just hope the s.o.b. never turns pro." Of course, Arnold went on to win the U.S. Amateur later that year, turned pro and changed the face of golf forever. (Modesty almost makes me neglect to mention that I won the Azalea in '54.)

The first time I played with Sam Snead was in the 1952 Jacksonville Open. He and Doug Ford and I were paired in the last group on Sunday. I misunderstood our tee time and was late getting to the course—since I was in contention, they sent the state police to escort me to the club. By the time I arrived, Snead and Ford had teed off and were playing the first hole. I hit off the first tee and ran down the fairway, taking a two-stroke penalty with me. When I reached the green, Sam came over with a big grin on his face, "What you been up to, Mouse?" he asked. "You can tell me her name, Mouse, huh?"

He kidded me all the way around. Then he got annoyed when I started outdriving him. "I'll get you, Mouse, if you keep jumpin' at it," he'd say. "You need some rocks in your pockets to stay on the ground, Mouse."

Finally, trying to keep up with him took its toll. I drove it out-of-bounds and dropped from contention. After that I made up my mind never to watch Snead swing when I played with him, because he hit it so pure and long I'd be coming out of my socks trying to stay with him. He'd always notice when I wasn't watching him, and he'd step away from the ball and say, "C'mon, Mouse, watch me swing?" Nowadays I never miss a chance to see that swing.

Almost 30 years later, Palmer is still winning tournaments, Snead is still knocking it past me, and I still need rocks in my pockets to keep up with them.